Dot

to

Dot

A novel by

L.G. Bradshaw

Dot to Dot
by L.G. Bradshaw

www.lgbradshaw.com

This book is a work of fiction. Names, characters, places, and incidents are the product of the author's imagination or are used fictitiously. Any resemblance to actual events, locales, or persons, living or dead, is coincidental.

International Standard Book Number: 1439266778

Cover design by Norman Michel Designs: www.naderkawas.com. Web site design by Eberhardt Tech Consulting: Eberhardt.jim@gmail.com.

ISBN-10: 1439266778
EAN-13: 9781439266779

Acknowledgements

None of us live in a vacuum. Consequently, no product, work of art or novel gets created without some kind of influence from others. I am indebted to so many wonderful people:

My sons, Michael and Andrew. Everything I do is done with you in mind.

Nader Kawas of *Norman Michel Designs* for creating an amazing cover.

Jim Eberhardt of *EberhardtTech Consulting* for his help getting my Web site up and running.

My parents, siblings, and friends, all of whom have provided much love, encouragement, and support through the years.

And, finally, many thanks to you, intrepid reader. If you like *Dot to Dot*, tell everyone you know and read my next novel. If you don't like it, read the next one anyway.

Thanks to Kevin Tildsley of Planetary Visions for use of the cover photo.

LGB

Colorado

1

Sex, Lies, And The Senator

The senior senator from Colorado spent the better part of the morning navigating the narrow, serpentine Tonahutu Lake Trail deep in the heart of Rocky Mountain National Park. The morning was postcard perfect—something John Denver might have written a song about before his nosedive into the Pacific. Had things been different the senator may have taken more time to appreciate the lush valleys and snowcapped peaks that surrounded him. As it was, things weren't different. They were bad. Very bad.

Despite what everyone was saying, he wasn't gay. The whole incident at the airport in North Carolina had been a huge misunderstanding. What happened after that was all the media's fault. The Democrats' too. They had both sensed blood in the water and attacked like frenzied sharks. Hypocrites. They were no better than him. Worse, in fact. They were the godless ones who championed abortion rights, gay marriage, and all sorts of other deviancy. Men wanting to marry other men. What was next? Men marrying sheep? Legalized incest? Marriage was sacred and was supposed to be one man and one woman. Those weren't his rules; they were God's. If it were up to him he'd round up every last queer, fag, lesbo, and dyke and dispose of them. They were perverse, unnatural. God had it right when he wiped Sodom and Gomorrah from the face of the earth. Too bad the cleansing didn't take. He remembered a few years back, right next door in Wyoming, when a couple of good old boys killed that fag Matthew Shepard. In the good senator's mind that hadn't been murder. That had been a community service killing. Those boys should have been given the Medal of Honor and immortalized on Mt. Rushmore's rocky tableau right next to Washington, Lincoln, Jefferson, and Roosevelt. None of them would have tolerated faggotry.

The beaten-down path narrowed farther along the spine of a minor peak, funneling through a granite gap and over a rocky outcrop. On the other side of the draw he emerged on the rim of a sprawling valley. In the far distance a herd of elk grazed contentedly in a meadow painted with a smear of yellow, purple and red flowers. Overhead, a pair of hawks pirouetted effortlessly, higher and higher until they were nothing more than mere specks against the deep blue canvas of sky. Five months from now this basin would be buried under fifteen feet of snow and colder than an icebox. But right now it was perfect. Serene, heavenly.

Twenty years. That's how long he had faithfully served the people of Colorado in the United States senate. Twenty years of arm-twisting, cajoling, and back-door deals that most people would never hear about. Two decades of fighting the good fight to make sure that America remained "One Nation Under God." Not "One Nation Under Planned Parenthood," or "One Nation Under Homosexuality." Under God. Under God! Now, his enemies wanted to undo all that hard work. To tarnish his legacy. He knew they would stop at nothing to destroy him. It was no big secret that the media had always been servants to the Left. So, when the story about his "activities" at the Raleigh-Durham International Airport came to light they pounced. Even though there was a perfectly logical, innocent explanation: the senator had a wide stance.

He tried setting the record straight numerous times. He had a wide stance when sitting on the toilet. His toe tapping wasn't some secret homosexual mating call, just a nervous tick. But no one would listen. Once the story made the news he knew he was cooked. He should have never paid the ticket. In doing so he basically admitted his guilt. At the time, all he wanted to do was make the mistake go away quickly and quietly. He wasn't guilty of anything more than being in the wrong place at the wrong time. He wanted to climb to the top of Pike's Peak and shout his innocence to the world. *I am not gay. I have never been gay.* He hated gays. Hated the disgusting thought of what they did with each other. But he couldn't say any of that either. His attorney had told him to keep his mouth shut. He told the senator that he would do all the talking.

This is how Jesus must have felt, he thought as he pushed on up the trail past a granite formation that looked almost phallic. Misunderstood. Persecuted for no good reason. Yes, that was it. He, Senator Dain Bramage, was just like Jesus Christ. Flogged and beaten by Pontius Pilate and forced down the Via Dolorosa with a tree trunk strapped across his shoulders. Only his Via Dolorosa was the marble-tiled gallery of Capitol Hill. His Pilate, the Democrats. His cross, the media.

He liked that thought. Maybe he could use it in a campaign speech once all of this blew over. And it would blow over, of that he was almost certain. He was the victim in this tragic melodrama. And it had all started with that brain-damaged queer in the airport. Too bad those good old boys in Wyoming hadn't gotten to him like they'd gotten Matthew Shepard. Too bad.

He scrambled up the apex of a smooth granite dome into a field exploding with daisies, wild strawberries, larkspur, and fireweed. An undulating sea of red, blue, yellow, and purple. Intermittent patches of snow dotted the ground, stubbornly refusing to give way to summer entirely.

Had he not been so focused on his latest round of tribulations, the senator might have seen the man half a mile back who had been tailing him since the beginning of his hike. As it was, he never noticed the rugged stranger.

• • •

Another half hour and he was in the clouds. They had materialized out of nowhere, boiling over the towering peaks in front of him, spilling down the valley like an advancing army of milky ghosts. Light drizzle fell, not soaking, but uncomfortable enough for him to don a camouflage Gore-Tex poncho. Up here, above the timberline, hypothermia could come without warning. Below the clouds, where he had started, it was in the low seventies. At twelve thousand five hundred feet it had cooled by more than twenty degrees. Not frigid, but it didn't have to be for hypothermia to settle in, disorient, and eventually kill you. Nature could be a fickle mistress. One minute she was luring you in with her siren song of breathtaking panoramas and amazing vistas. The next, she was trying to kill you.

He didn't plan on falling for any of her capricious tricks today. As a former Navy SEAL, the assassin was well acquainted with the outdoors. In fact, he fancied himself another Bear Grylls, just without the TV show. Like him, Grylls was a former military man. Unlike Grylls, however, the assassin's post-military career didn't involve mugging for the camera while chewing on plump, foot-long

Burmese millipedes. Sure, he could do that—had done that. Many times, actually.

Growing up, his father used to tell him that a man would eat rocks if he was hungry enough. While he had never actually eaten rocks on an operation, he had consumed other things that would make a billy goat puke. Once, after lying camouflaged for a week in a miasmatic swamp on the outskirts of Panama City, he decided to sample some of the local delicacies. He liked the agaveworms the best. They were the size of his thumb and had flooded his mouth with a sweet, nutty crunch. Bird-eating spiders weren't bad, but he wasn't a big fan of Central American termites. Too bitter.

Had the money not been so good he would never have accepted this job. It wasn't that he was opposed to neutralizing elected officials. He'd done it before, mainly overseas though in third world hellholes with little centralized government and inept or nonexistent law enforcement. His most recent job had been six months earlier in Nigeria. A local warlord, Mohammed something or other, had suddenly decided that he no longer wanted to be the CIA's lapdog. This, despite having been happy to take more than fifty thousand American dollars from the agency for taking out local militants.

In Nigeria that was more than the average person would make in a lifetime. It was also the equivalent of being fabulously wealthy: an entire herd of goats, five hundred camels, two thousand chickens, and a thousand acres of barren African soil. Oh, and five wives, all of whom were held in lower esteem than the chickens.

Unfortunately for the Nigerian, his alleged targets kept turning up alive in such distant outposts as Iraq and Afghanistan. As a result, the CIA decided it was time to terminate the warlord's employment. So they placed a call.

Forty-eight hours later an unseen sniper's round fired from nearly a mile away tore through Mohammed something or other's right eye, leaving an exit wound the size of a grapefruit at the back of his head and half of his brains splattered on the side of a rusty tin shack. Dead before hitting the ground, the warlord entered the afterlife disappointed that the forty virgins he'd been promised weren't there waiting for him.

Ten minutes after firing the fatal round, the assassin was in a safe house on the outskirts of Abuja. An hour after that he was on his way back to the States traveling with his forged passport and assumed name. He'd come up with the alias years earlier after pondering the etiology of his favorite band's name, and wondering what the exact opposite would be. That day, Mr. A.A. Bottom was born.

The CIA weren't the only ones who utilized his services. Other arms of government, both foreign and domestic, kept his secure number on speed dial as well. It wasn't that he particularly enjoyed killing. He wasn't a psychopath. There was a big difference between him and the Ted Bundys of the world. He killed purely for profit, and because he could do it without compunction. Ted Bundy and men like him killed because they enjoyed it—needed it on some primitive, psychosexual level. Bottom didn't need it, and he never made it personal. It was always about only one thing: business. And his business worked like this.

A cryptic message sent to a secure Web address. Half the money up front, deposited into an offshore account, half deposited upon completion of the job. Really, it was pretty simple. He had never been one for too much cloak-and-dagger stuff. That didn't mean he wasn't cautious. He just believed that convoluted plots or instructions created too much confusion. Confusion led to hesitation, and hesitation led to mission failure. And that was one thing he couldn't tolerate, from himself or others. So far, after nearly six years in the business, he was batting a thousand. Nine jobs, nine targets neutralized. And today, Colorado Senator Dain Bramage would be number ten. This time tomorrow he would be one million dollars richer and exactly halfway to his retirement goal.

When he first started in this business A.A. Bottom promised himself two things: never kill an innocent person and do only twenty hits. So far, he had kept his first rule intact. All the people he had neutralized had it coming one way or another. Senator Dain Bramage was no exception. He was a loudmouth prick who had ruffled the political feathers of some very powerful people. People who had no qualms about contacting someone like Bottom and paying handsomely for his unique services. "Accidents" happened all the time in politics. Like the time Unites States Senator Paul Wellstone's plane crashed in Northern Minnesota. He had been a loudmouth too.

Despite his insistence that none of this was ever personal, the assassin had to admit that this time things were a bit different. Just a bit.

He'd done his research on the senator, just like he'd done with every past mark. Thorough investigations prevented him from taking out someone who didn't deserve it. That was one thing he couldn't live with.

The senator had been caught by an undercover cop at the Raleigh-Durham International Airport having sex with another man in one of the bathroom stalls. Bottom actually felt sorry for the other guy. He'd been a lawyer, married with two young kids, who'd suffered a brain injury after falling off his roof while stringing up Christmas lights. After coming out of a week-long coma, the true extent of the lawyer's injuries became evident. His personality had changed completely. Quiet and thoughtful before, he became prone to violent, erratic outbursts. Something else about him changed too. Something more fundamental.

The lawyer became gay.

Not just gay in the sense of preferring men over women. Flamingly, flamboyantly gay, prancing around in public wearing outlandish clothing, feather boas, and spike heeled shoes. He also started frequenting public bathrooms and engaging in the *Tea Room Trade*.

Tea Room Trade? Never heard of that, so he dug a little more.

In 1970, Laud Humphreys published his doctoral thesis, *Tearoom Trade*. Tea rooming was the term used for anonymous male-on-male sexual encounters, generally in public places like restrooms. Humphreys interviewed men who engaged in this type of behavior and found that they came from all sorts of socioeconomic backgrounds. Doctors, lawyers, cops, janitors, teachers. Half of them considered themselves "straight," and had unsuspecting wives waiting for them at home. Humphreys also found that many of these men camouflaged their activities by hiding behind a shield of sorts. A "Breastplate of Righteousness," as he called it, that helped them psychologically reconcile the differences between their public lives and the deviant subculture of bathroom sex trawlers. Now, the senior senator from Colorado made sense.

Still, it didn't do the poor lawyer in North Carolina any good. The publicity generated by the arrest pushed him over the edge. He ended up committing suicide a month later by jumping off the Mainline Bridge on the outskirts of Raleigh.

That's what made part of this hit personal. Bottom knew that his older brother had been a good man before becoming a victim of circumstance and his own mutinous mind. But the senator from Colorado had been disingenuous and terribly unkind. The assassin's brother couldn't help what he had become; the senator didn't have that excuse. If he had, things would be vastly different. He wouldn't be about to perish in a tragic hiking accident on the Tonahutu Lake Trail in Rocky Mountain National Park. At least not at the hands of Mr. A.A. Bottom.

• • •

After another thousand feet of elevation, the senator was almost there. One hundred yards ahead lay his final destination, crystalline and glimmering in the filtered sunlight: Tonahutu Lake, a glacial basin nestled snugly in the saddle of two jagged peaks.

This was his fortress of solitude. The place he came to twice a month to recharge his batteries. No matter how ugly things got down below in the real world he could always count on the rarified air up here to clear his thoughts. He needed it now more than ever.

Technically speaking, the hike was not difficult or demanding. A gentle, gradual rise in elevation punctuated by a few rocky outcrops you had to scramble over. Near the summit the severely constricted ribbon of trail threaded through the Eye of the Needle, a smooth stone arch perched on the razor's edge of a thousand-foot drop. Just past that was Diamond Falls, a twenty-foot-high cascade of snowmelt that hugged the side of the mountain and emptied into a bubbling creek that knifed through the valley below.

On a normal, clear day he could make it from the parking lot to the lake in three hours. It had taken a bit longer this morning because of the soupy cloud cover two thousand feet below, but that was to be expected from time to time. Still, three and a half hours

wasn't too bad for a man approaching sixty. He bet there were people half his age who couldn't do it given twice the time.

The best part was that he rarely encountered other hikers up
here. The more popular trails were shorter and relegated to the
lower elevations. This one was secluded and much less traveled.
Perfect for the solitude he craved sometimes. Perfect, also, for getting away from his shrew of a wife.

Their marriage had been a sham. A carefully orchestrated political maneuver to ensure his electability. The only thing she really
cared about was the notoriety and stature his position brought to
her. Frankly, that didn't bother him. She was nothing more than arm
candy and the vessel that had brought two more political props into
the world: son Michael and daughter Mallory. He thought he loved
them. If nothing else, he at least liked them. Tolerated them?

Actually, now that he really thought about it, he couldn't stand
them either. They were snotty, distant, and completely spoiled, just
like their mother. But they all looked great posed together for campaign photos. Having the All-American Family gave him some of
the cache he needed to further his political career. Beautiful wife
(physically, at least), blonde-haired, blue-eyed kids who could have
subbed for child models in any print or TV ad. They had their mother's lithe, athletic figure and his chiseled good looks. Their pair-
ing had been a killer combination, genetically and on the campaign
trail. At least the shrew had been good for something other than
shopping and spending all his money.

He stopped at the edge of the lake and eased his pack to the
ground. His lower back throbbed lightly and his feet ached but it
was all worth it. He had the shimmering glacial pool and surrounding peaks all to himself. Nearby, a smooth boulder beckoned so he
took a seat. Inside his backpack was lunch: a bag of trail mix, heavy

on the M&M's, peanut butter and jelly sandwich, and a lukewarm can of soda. Ten minutes submerged in the lake and the Coke would be ice cold, just the way he liked it.

The senator loosened the laces on his hiking boots, adjusted his socks and rubbed his feet. He had an hour before he'd have to start back down. Sunset came early in the mountains and he didn't want to be stuck on the trail after that. He knew this trail like the back of his hand, but navigating it in the dark would be suicide.

• • •

Two hundred yards away, tucked behind a cairn of dark rocks, the assassin watched. He hadn't seen anyone else on the trail all morning and that was good. He didn't believe in collateral damage, especially on an operation like this. On the battlefield, that was one thing. But out here, unacceptable. If an innocent compromised the job he would simply abort. It didn't appear that he'd be doing that today.

He watched the senator drop a can of soda in the lake, retie his boot laces and dig into his lunch. The sandwich was gone in four quick bites, followed by a handful of something he pulled from a plastic Ziploc. Probably trail mix. The assassin had a bag of his own in his backpack. Much better than the worms, spiders, and termites he'd eaten in Panama.

If the senator suspected anything he didn't let on. Bottom figured Bramage was blissfully unaware he was being followed. That would make things easier.

Then, out of nowhere, things got really easy.

• • •

"Goddamn fags!" The senator's shouted words echoed across the valley. "Screw all of you. I hope you all burn in hell!"

The senator stood, grabbed his backpack and started pinwheeling it into the ground. Then, he stopped, sat back down on the boulder, and buried his head in his hands, weeping uncontrollably.

Startled, Bottom retrained his binoculars on the mark. He watched as the senator again stood and kicked his pack ten feet down a gentle incline. The guy was losing it, psychologically disintegrating right before his very eyes. Had it been anyone else, Bottom would have felt sorry for him. He felt no such pity for the senator. The man had made his bed, and now he had to lie in it.

• • •

Get ahold of yourself, Senator.

The voice was calm yet insistent. It was a sound he had become very familiar with over the years. His voice, but not the vocalized version. This one lurked somewhere in the shadowy recesses of his mind.

"Leave me alone." The senator's reply was a dry, dusty croak. He didn't need this. Not right now. All he wanted was a few uninterrupted hours of peace. That's why he had come up here. A reprieve from the voice. *His* voice.

You know I can't do that. The voice chuckled wickedly. *You may think you can run and hide from everyone else, but you can't hide from me. You never could. Especially when Uncle Ted used to make you do those disgusting things to him when you were six.*

"Stop it! Shut up!"

No, you stop it. Stop acting like a pussy. I'm not the one who's losing it; you are. I'm just here to make sure you don't forget about who you really are.

"I know who I am," the senator replied. The whimpering note of uncertainty in his voice betrayed him though. "I'm the senior senator from Colorado. Chair of the finance committee and assistant chair for the oversight committee."

More snide laughter. *You're also a queer, Dain, old boy. And now, everyone knows it. Finally, we can be together. Just embrace your true self. Let's take that leap of faith together. Then you can stop fucking strangers in public bathrooms.*

"I don't do that. That was all a mistake. A misunderstanding..."

The voice didn't let him finish. *You can't fool me, Senator. You forget, I know everything about you. You just want to deal with how you see yourself. I'm all about dealing with the real you. The person you keep hidden in the shadows, away from the sunlight. The person who likes sucking dick in dirty bathroom stalls.*

"That's disgusting. I don't do that!" the senator screamed, causing a growl that sounded like a feral beast to echo through the valley.

Still in denial. Well, that's why I'm here. To keep you honest and never lose sight of your true self. Wasn't it Shakespeare who said, "To thine own self be true"? You may be high above the clouds now, away from the real world down there, but you can't run away from yourself, Senator. Your days of running are over.

. . .

Thirty yards away now and Bottom could hear everything the senator was saying. The politician was rambling incoherently, literally having a running dialogue with someone who wasn't there. It had to be one of the strangest things he'd seen in a long time.

The strangest thing he'd ever seen had been in Tijuana a couple years back: a young girl, probably no more than fourteen, having sex with a donkey. The nauseating show hadn't been his idea. He had followed his mark, a Mexican drug cartel kingpin, into the spuzzy sex bar, learning the man's patterns and habits. The next day he took the kingpin out, mainly to avoid having to see another live donkey sex show. He felt sorry for the girl. The donkey too. Where was PETA when you really needed them? Or PETH, for that matter? People for the Ethical Treatment of Humans.

He was about to inch closer to the senator when it happened. At first, he wasn't sure he was seeing things correctly. Then, in an instant of recognition, he knew what was about to happen. He contemplated his next move and decided that doing nothing was the best option. The senator would do all the hard work for him.

• • •

The rest happened in an unceremonious blur. The senator stood, closed his eyes for a moment, stretched out his arms and cocked his head skyward. Then, he ran from the lake, faster and faster. He seemed to be almost floating above the ground as he approached the cliff. An instant later he was gone, plunging headlong over the side like a tumbling rag doll, screaming about God, fags, and eternal damnation all the way down to the bottom of the craggy gorge.

Then, silence.

Bottom didn't run from his concealed location. He never ran unless bullets were flying or things around him were exploding. But he did move quickly, cautiously to where he had just seen the senior senator from Colorado make his spectacular swan dive. At the edge he trained his binoculars on the uneven terrain below. He caught site of the body at the bottom of the thousand-foot drop, bloody and broken on a mantel of serrated granite. Overhead, large birds were already circling, greedily eyeing the shredded carrion below. A feast like this didn't come along that often.

Mission accomplished, the assassin thought as he took one last look at the senator's body and then turned back down the trail. Probably the easiest five hundred thousand dollars he would ever make. Although it was already spent, so he wouldn't have it for long. All the funds from this job were going to three people who needed it more than he. He hoped the money would bring some measure of peace and security to his brother's wife and two kids in North Carolina. After everything they'd been through recently, they deserved at least that much.

2

The Senator's Wife

At the funeral, the senator's wife did her best to comfort the children. She wished she had someone to comfort her. The past few months had been a living hell. Ever since reports of that "thing" in North Carolina broke, their personal lives had become an open book. "Sex, Lies, and the Senator." That's the headline one prominent magazine had splashed across its front cover, along with a photo of her husband, smiling like a politician and giving a thumbs-up at some political rally. The editors decided to get cute by superimposing half a dozen small lipstick prints across his face. Only in her husband's case the lipstick kisses would have been placed there by a man.

The thought of that made Jane Bramage want to gag. How long had he been leading his secret life? She didn't know for sure, but everything she'd read told her that it had been going on for years. Still, she had no clue until the story appeared in the *Denver Post*. Then, like a disease, it spread, until it was the lead story on every local and national media outlet. Sex might sell, but gay bathroom sex by prominent politicians was even more bankable.

Where did I go wrong? she thought as the honor guard folded the coffin flag into a tight triangle. Two soldiers handed the folded flag to her. With mechanical precision they offered a sharp salute, turned, and slowly marched back into position. Ten-year-old Michael seemed mesmerized by the military men; Mallory simply sat in her mother's lap, not really sure what was going on. At six, she was old enough to know that her father was gone. Jane wasn't sure she understood the permanence of his absence.

"Will daddy be back for Christmas?" Mallory asked as she leaned in and whispered into her mother's ear.

Jane smiled sadly and shook her head. "I'm afraid not, sweetie," she said softly. "Daddy's in heaven now."

The lie tasted bitter in her mouth. She didn't believe for a second that Dain Bramage had ascended to a higher plane. He had been a miserable husband and father. Mean spirited, sarcastic, impatient, quick to anger, and impossible to please. Still, it was hard to completely hate the man. Without him she wouldn't have her children, the two most precious things in her world. Now, her world had gotten a bit smaller.

Actually, that wasn't entirely true. Her world, especially after the wedding, had always been small. Dain had wooed her only for her looks and notoriety as a former Ms. New Mexico and Ms. America runner-up. She knew that now. Looking back on things, she wasn't sure he ever really loved her. At least not in the way a man should love a woman. The only person he really loved was himself. After that came his career. His wife and kids were further down the list. She wondered if they ever even made the list at all.

The rest of the graveside service went by in a blur. Not because she was terribly sad at having lost Dain. She had lost him long ago.

Probably never even had him. It went by in a blur because she was thinking about the future. A future free of *him*. A future spent raising her children the way she saw fit: lots of hugs and kisses, bedtime stories, trips to the park, bike rides, Disneyland, picnics, the zoo, watching movies at home with a big bowl of butter-soaked popcorn. All things that Dain never had time for. Or, more accurately, never *made* time for. Simple things that made life worth living.

She realized long ago that it was the simple things in life that were the most important. Bigger houses, fancier cars, exotic vacations, more money, and power. Those things were fine, but they weren't what made life special. Relationships were important. A beautiful sunrise and blazing sunset, important. A walk through a mountain meadow on a warm summer day, that was important. Funny, the older she got, the more she savored those simple things. They were truly the spice of life. Not that she was the wife of an important man, or wore the Ms. America crown.

At the reception hall she finally came to life, working the crowd like she used to at all of Dain's political functions. This was her element. Pressing the flesh and making people feel good. She'd always had that effect on people. It was a gift, she supposed. Most of the time anyway.

She hadn't felt that spark today until now. With the cemetery and burial behind her she felt…liberated? Yes, that was it. Liberated from the fake life she had been living for the past ten years. A plastic existence made up entirely of being the wife of a senator. In that whole process she had lost herself—who she really was. The only things that kept her grounded, kept her real during that time, were Michael and Mallory. They had been her anchor. She knew that now. It was her turn to return the favor.

• • •

Handshakes and hugs all around the room. Phrases like "he was a good man," and "such a tragic loss," and "he's looking down on us right now," circulated through the crowd of mourners.

They obviously didn't know the *real* Dain Bramage. But how could they? Like a diamond, he had many different sides to him, most of them phony and directed toward maintaining his career and image. Unlike a diamond, there wasn't much shiny or precious about him.

Another hug by someone she didn't know, paired with hollow platitudes whispered in her ear. She didn't think she could take anymore. All she wanted to do was grab her children and leave. Hop in the car and speed back to the solitude of their mountain retreat in Estes Park.

"He was the best, Jane. The absolute best." The meaningless words came from a man she'd met before—what was his name? She couldn't recall. He was tall, neatly dressed in a dark three-piece suit and had an air of authority about him. It came to her an instant later. Dan Simmons. The lobbyist from Merrick Davis, the pharmaceutical giant. That was it.

"Thanks, Dan," she as she nodded and smiled somberly. "He was something all right."

"If you and the kids need anything, anything at all, please don't hesitate to call," Simmons said. He leaned in and took her in his arms. "I know how hard this can be."

Awkwardly, she returned the embrace. She began to feel uncomfortable just a few moments later after the hug lingered longer than it should have.

Simmons pulled her in even closer and whispered in her ear. "I'm here for you, Jane. Whatever you need."

His breath came out in a warm pant. Did he just lick her ear?

She pulled away abruptly and stepped back. "Thanks again, Dan. We'll be fine." Curt and clipped. She may not have loved her husband, but coming onto her at the man's funeral. God, that was beyond tacky. It was lecherous, creepy, and it made her want to throw up. Were all men single-minded pigs? She was starting to wonder.

Jane whirled and pulled the kids toward the exit. They didn't complain. Maybe all the phony, syrupy accolades had finally gotten to them too. They knew the kind of man their father really was. Sometimes, kids were more perceptive than adults. Or at least more genuine, she thought.

"Poor woman," a faceless voice muttered from the humming gallery as they made their escape. "She's just lost her whole reason for living."

She almost laughed out loud. If only they knew her real reasons for living were leaving with her right now. And very soon, they would be leaving Colorado for good. She'd call her cousin first thing tomorrow. He owned *A-1 Moving*, one of the largest moving companies in the mountain west. After this nightmare she wanted out of Colorado. Back to New Mexico, she thought. Back to her roots and a simpler life.

3

The Movers

"Pussy is overrated."

Chuck Roswell's words hung in the air like a slowly deflating balloon before the inevitable came.

"What are you talking about?" Tim Bisbee spoke first, wide-eyed and incredulous. "Come on, Chuck, you're not a homo. Are you?"

Chuck cast a sideways glance at the youngest and newest member of his crew. He leaned back against the plywood wall of the half-empty moving truck, peeled a peanut butter and mayonnaise sandwich from its Saran Wrap skin and took a bite.

"What do you think?" He chewed three times and washed the masticated mush down with two large gulps of Pepsi. A playful smirk pulled at the corners of his mouth.

Eighteen-year-old Tim, fresh out of high school and working his first "real" job, glanced nervously back and forth. First at Chuck, then around the three other movers—Adonis Boyd, Jeff Carter, Paco—and then back at Chuck. He couldn't remember Paco's last name but thought there was a Lopez or Rodriguez somewhere in there.

"Naw, you're messing with me, man," Timmy finally said and grinned. The uncertainty on his boyish face drained away, at least partially.

Chuck took another bite, leaned forward and propped his elbows atop his kneecaps. Instead of speaking he stared at the young mover. After a few uncomfortable moments of silence he laughed out loud and reached over and cuffed Timmy on the back.

"No, I'm not a *homo*, as you so eloquently put it," Chuck said. "Completely straight. Always have been, always will be. Unless I get a traumatic brain injury somewhere along the way and suddenly come out of my coma craving men. It's been known to happen."

"No way, man." Adonis Boyd spoke this time. "How can that happen?"

Adonis was from the south side of Chicago. His mother had been a crackhead and his father left the family when he was two. His grandmother basically raised him, especially after his momma went to prison for helping murder a crack whore in a park bathroom. Beat her to half to death with a wrench. When she didn't die right away Adonis' mom and her pimp/accomplice/boyfriend tortured the poor girl, cutting off her breasts while she was still alive. Then, they shoved a large, jagged tree branch up her vagina so far that it ended up puncturing the young whore's heart. He found out all this years later after reading copies of the police report. All his grandmother ever told him was that his mother had made some bad choices in her life. No kidding.

"It most certainly can happen," Chuck replied. "It's been documented numerous times in medical journals. In fact, from what I've read in the newspapers, that's why we're doing this move to Las Cruces."

A puzzled look from the new guy, followed by, "What do you mean?"

"Turns out the woman we're moving is the wife of Senator Bramage," Chuck explained. "You know the story. They found his body in the mountains. Suicide, I guess. He jumped off a thousand-foot cliff. Birds and scavengers ate most of him up before they found him."

"I remember hearing about that," Jeff Carter chimed in. "Didn't he get caught doing nasty things in some airport bathroom?"

Chuck nodded.

"That's what I understand. An undercover cop caught him and some other guy in the act. Turns out the other guy had some sort of brain injury. Before all that he'd been happily married for ten years with two kids. He was on the roof stringing Christmas lights up when he lost his footing. Landed square on his head. He pulled, but he was never the same. Turns out the brain damage didn't make him a vegetable; it turned him gay. He started frequenting the international airport, in fact, hanging out in the bathrooms and having sex with complete strangers. Very bizarre."

"How come you know so much about this?" Tim asked.

"Old boy used to be a doctor," Adonis piped in, thumbing in Chuck's direction. "We got ourselves a real, bona fide M.D. here. Comes in real handy when you drop a dresser on your foot."

"You used to be a doctor?" Tim asked, a mix of awe and puzzlement in his voice.

Chuck nodded but said nothing.

"Well?" Tim said.

"Well, what?"

Tim stood and stretched his slender legs. "What happened? I mean, you're a relocation supervisor for A-1 Movers, now. How did you go from doctor to mover? Seems like kind of a big step backwards to me."

Chuck laughed but there was no humor in his voice. "Long story, kid."

"We've got time," Jeff Carter interjected. Carter was a former Marine who had served two tours of duty in Iraq.

Chuck glanced at his watch. They had a few more minutes left of their lunch break. Why not dazzle young Tim with his tales of incompetence. After all, the rest of the guys knew.

"Paco, what do you think? Want to hear the story of my demise again?"

Paco shrugged. "It's OK." It sounded more like "*Eeess hokay,*" his standard reply when he didn't fully understand what was going on.

Chuck had hired Paco Gomez Rodriguez Bonilla Lopez three weeks earlier and he'd proven to be a good mover. Paco's papers said he was from Juarez, Mexico, just on the other side of El Paso. According to his documents, everything was in order. Chuck had asked him how he'd decided on Colorado as a final destination. The Mexican simply shrugged. Chuck asked him if he knew any English. He shrugged again.

"*Muy poco*—very little," Paco replied. "Cocksucker, mother-fucker, shit, bitch. Pizza?"

Chuck hired Paco after his laughing fit subsided. The Mexican would fit into his crew just fine.

"Wait,"Timmy interrupted. "Before you go into all that, I wanna know what you meant when you said pussy's overrated. No offense, boss, but that sounds like kind of a fag thing to say."

Chuck grimaced theatrically and then laughed. "Tim, you have a way with words. I love it! So genuine and uninhibited. Real salt of the earth."

The newest member of the crew shrugged uncertainly. He didn't understand what the big deal was. All he wanted to know was whether or not his boss was gay. He didn't think that was asking too much. Frankly, he mostly didn't even care. Ninety percent didn't care—maybe eighty. For the most part he believed that what a man did with his private parts was his own business. Stick 'em in a girl, stick 'em in a guy. Hell, stick 'em in a tree for all he cared. Still, there was that unaccounted for ten or twenty percent that persistently nagged that gays were doomed to the fiery furnace of hell if they didn't change their ways. That was his Catholic up-bringing talking. Homosexuality was an aberration, an abomination in the eyes of God. His parents had drilled that into him from an early age. Fags were evil. Fags were cursed souls doomed for all eternity to suffer every perverted form of indignity in the sulfury bowels of Hades. All because they liked penis over vagina. When he really thought about it, eternal damnation seemed like kind of a high price to pay for that. Didn't God have better things to worry about?

"OK," Chuck finally continued. "I can see how a virile, obviously heterosexual young man like you could be perplexed by what I said. What I meant was this: sex—with the female vagina being the most symbolic interpretation of that act for men— is pretty much the same no matter where you go or who you sleep with. Men have been getting themselves in trouble since the dawn of time because of that thing. And for what? A few tingling moments of pleasure in your loins? Then, after a while, a guy gets bored with the same piece of ass. So what does he do?"

No one answered.

"I'll tell you what he does," Chuck continued. "He goes looking for another piece thinking it's going to be better than the last piece. Only it's not. After a while, he gets tired of that too. Because, when you get right down to it, all pussy is the same. There are only so many different ways you can flip someone over. Once you've explored all those ways what else is there?"

Another pause with another stretch of rhetorical silence.

"Well, then you start looking for the next *different* piece of ass. It's really a vicious cycle. Once the initial excitement wears off you get bored and start searching for the next exciting thing. Only the next exciting thing soon becomes worn out, like an old pair of shoes."

"So, what you're saying is that pussy is like an old pair of shoes?" Jeff stood and cracked his back. "Maybe I should dump my girlfriend and screw my Nikes."

A low chuckle rippled through the group.

"Yeah, I guess that's what I'm saying," Chuck said absently, not really hearing the last part of what the former Marine said. "An old pair of shoes that you love at first. Clean, comfortable. You wear them all the time, beat the hell out of them, and pretty soon they look nothing like the shoes you fell in love with."

This time Chuck didn't smile. His eyes dropped and remained fixed on an oily stain on the scuffed wooden floor of the semitrailer.

"That's my life, now" Chuck mumbled under his breath, barely audibly. "A pair of worn-out old shoes."

"What did you say?" Jeff Carter queried.

Chuck lifted his gaze, snapping back to reality. "Oh...sorry, nothing. Just thinking about an old pair of shoes I used to have. A really nice pair that I wish I still had..."

4

A Pantheon of Family Heroes

Jeff Carter's great grandfather killed Germans in trenches during World War I. Thomas Carter ended up in those muddy troughs all because some Serbian fanatic shot and killed Austrian Arch Duke Franz Ferdinand in 1914. Unfortunately, after millions of casualties, the Great War never took. Someone obviously forgot to tell a young German soldier that it was billed as the war to end all wars. Either that, or Adolph Hitler just didn't care for the moniker.

During World War II Jeff's grandfather fought the Japanese, leapfrogging from island to bloody island in the South Pacific until President Harry S. Truman decided to end things once and for all by dropping *Little Boy* and *Fat Man* on Hiroshima and Nagasaki. His grandfather told him that more than two hundred thousand people were killed in those bombings, and he couldn't have been happier.

"Those two horrible nuclear bombs probably saved me," he once told Jeff. "It was either that, or we were going to send millions of troops ashore and storm Japan. That wouldn't have been pretty. For us, or them."

Twenty-five years after *Little Boy* and *Fat Man* saved his grandfather's life, Jeff's dad humped his way through the bush in Southeast Asia killing gooks, dinks, slopes, and/or Victor Charlie. They used things called Willie Pete, Bouncing Bettys, beehive rounds, napalm, and claymores. They said things like *sin loi*, *beau coup*, *caca dau*, and FNG. They did things like pop smoke, Zippo raids, medevacs and extractions.

And they fought and died in places none of them had ever heard of before arriving in the fetid jungles of Vietnam: Ia Drang. Phu Bai. Da Lat.

So, when the second airliner slammed into the World Trade Center on September 11, 2001, Jeff knew his time had come to help preserve freedom and democracy. He didn't even hesitate or think about it. He walked into the nearest recruiting station and enlisted. Four years. United States Marine Corps. Infantry.

Now, he could be included in the pantheon of family heroes: Thomas Carter, United States Army. James Carter, United States Marine Corps. John Carter, United States Army. And finally, him, Jeff Carter, United States Marine Corps. He had no idea on what far-off plain his war would be fought, but wherever they wanted to send him he was ready. He just had no idea how hot, dusty, and desolate Iraq would be. Or how much damage a roadside bomb could do to the human body.

• • •

"Just remember one thing. In combat, there's no such thing as a coward."

They were at the airport. Jeff, dress blues neatly pressed and creased, brass buffed to a high sheen, duffel bag slung over one shoulder. Behind him loomed the gaping maw of the Jetway; in front of him stood his parents. Mom cried softly, dad tried not to.

The elder Carter knew that war was hell. He'd seen combat, killed men. Some innocent, some not. But sending your son off to a similar hell—that was far worse. If the Corps would have let him he'd have gladly traded places with Jeff right then and there.

"I know, Dad," Jeff nodded. "You've told me that before."

"Yeah, well, just want to make sure you heard me," John Carter muttered. He glanced at the floor and mindlessly toed a ripped scab of carpet. "Oh, and keep..."

Jeff finished the sentence for him. "*Keep your head down and your powder dry*. I've heard that one too, Dad."

This time he smiled reassuringly, more for their benefit than his own. He was going to be fine. He'd told them that a thousand times. This was all going to be over quickly, just like in 1991. With their superior numbers and equipment they would roll up the Iraqi army and Republican Guard like an old rug and win over the hearts and minds of the Iraqi people in no time.

He wasn't certain that his parents bought into his confident act. Hell, he wasn't sure that *he* really bought into it either. War was never that cut and dried. And no war was ever the same as the one that came before.

His mother started to say something but the words wouldn't come. All she could manage was a tangled mess of sobs as she wrapped her arms around her son's neck. Finally, she muttered something softly into his ear: "I love you, Jeff. You will always be my little boy."

He almost lost it there. He caught himself before the tears came, returned the embrace and mumbled that he loved her too and that he promised he would be careful. He turned toward the Jetway but his father grabbed him by the arm.

"Here, take this," John Carter said. He reached into his pocket and pressed something cool and metallic into his son's palm.

Jeff knew what it was instantly. He didn't have to look at his father's most cherished possession, after his wife and kids. The younger Carter nodded and stuffed the cool piece of tin in his pocket. He turned and boarded the plane bound for North Carolina and then Iraq. Somewhere over Tennessee he finally pulled the out the old Army dog tag and glanced at the raised lettering of a name he'd heard from his father many times. The name of a man who had saved John Carter's life in Vietnam thirty-five years earlier. His real name was Thomas R. Stinson, but his dad always called him *Chickenman*.

5

In the Zone

"Jeff, hello. Hello…"

Jeff Carter heard his name and looked up at Chuck. "Yeah."

"Dude, I called your name like five times," Chuck said from outside the truck. "You were in the zone again."

Jeff looked around and noticed he was the only one left in the truck. The others had gathered in a cluster outside and were wrestling with a blocky armoire. The armoire looked like it was winning.

"Oh, sorry," Jeff muttered. He shook his head slightly, stood, and glanced at his watch. Twenty minutes had passed. "I didn't hear a thing."

"I know. You were really gone this time."

Chuck mounted the dented iron tailgate and clambered into the back of the semitrailer. He brushed a misshapen patch of rusty silt off his khaki shorts and plopped down next to Jeff.

"You OK?"

Jeff nodded slowly. "Yeah, I'm fine. Sorry for spacing out like that."

"Don't sweat it," Chuck replied. "I just wonder where you go when you're in the zone like that."

Jeff glanced over at his boss and laughed. "Far from here," he said. "It's not always the same place. Sometimes I'm back in Iraq, sometimes I'm back in my childhood."

A thoughtful nod, followed by, "Where were you today?"

Most of the time Jeff didn't like sharing his thoughts with others. They didn't understand—couldn't understand. To them war was just something they read about in history books or saw clips of on the evening news or the History Channel. War wasn't real. It was distant, a flash of chaos on TV or a blurb in the newspaper. To him, though, it had been real. Deadly real.

"I was back in the airport leaving for my first tour in Iraq," Jeff finally said. He reached up and brushed an errant strand of dark hair from his eyes. "My parents were there with me when I left. Man, that was hard."

Chuck nodded and remained silent. He had never served in the military, never been in a combat zone. The closest he had come to combat was working the ER at Cook County Hospital in Chicago during his residency. Now that he thought about it, that place had been a war zone. He should have received hazard pay for working there. Maybe even a Purple Heart.

"Then," Jeff continued, "I started thinking about the *Chickenman*."

Chuck cocked a sideways glance at the former Marine. A puzzled look filled the lines on his face. "OK, I'll bite," he said after it became clear that his partner wasn't going to offer an immediate explanation. "Who is the *Chickenman*?"

Jeff told him.

6

The Chickenmen

They were all *Chickenmen*. That's what the Vietnamese in the village of Bao Dai called anyone who wore the Screaming Eagle shoulder patch of the 101st Airborne. Tony Miller who hailed from Los Angeles. Robert Samuels from New Jersey. John Carter, Cleveland.

Vietnam had a lot of things. Malarial mosquitoes, vipers, a prosperous black market drug trade, and cheap whores. And, perhaps most distressing, a seemingly endless supply of young men who would materialize out of the jungle in their black pajamas, lay an ambush and then melt back into the suffocating foliage like phantoms. But one thing they didn't have was the bald eagle.

The winged symbol of American might did not exist in Vietnam. It was a predatory bird confined to the spacious skies and fruited plains of North America. So, when the Vietnamese first encountered the troopers from the 101st Airborne, they had no frame of reference for the bird sewn onto their shoulders. The closest thing they could compare it to was the chicken. Naturally, the men who wore those patches were *Chickenmen*.

The name stuck.

There may have been a lot of *Chickenmen* during the Screaming Eagles' tenure in Vietnam, but there was only one true *Chickenman*: Tommy Stinson from La Grange, Texas, a dusty burg midway between Austin and Houston immortalized in song a few years later by *tres hombres* known as ZZ Top. Had he lived, Tommy would have liked the song.

Bespectacled and bookish, Stinson looked more like an accountant than a member of an elite fighting force. Soaking wet he may have topped out at one thirty, not much more than the ruck and gear he humped day in and day out through the soggy jungles and mist-camouflaged valleys of South Vietnam. But what he lacked in size, Stinson made up for with an overinflated amount of courage. And an equally inflated amount of humility.

"I'm no hero," he would say in letters sent back home. "Just doing my job."

That's the way all of the Chickenmen saw things. They weren't heroes—there wasn't much heroic in having to kill other men. They simply had a job to do, so they did it. Begrudgingly, sometimes, but they did it nonetheless. And Tommy Stinson seemed to do his job better than just about anyone else, considering the meager physical attributes he'd been given.

•   •   •

The Screaming Eagles weren't supposed to be in Hue city in June of 1971. In fact, no American troops should have been there.

All operations in that part of South Vietnam had been turned over to ARVN forces in a gradual pullback by the American military. People back home in the States were tired of the daily grind of grim war news, mounting casualties, and filled body bags. America wanted its sons out of Vietnam. Those sons would have been happy to oblige.

One thing the men of the 101st knew well, however, was that there was a big difference between where you *should* be and where you actually *were*. As far as they were concerned, none of them *should* have been in Vietnam. Let the South Vietnamese fight their own battles. Yet, here they *were*. So, when the Navy swift boat dropped the four men from Bravo platoon on the banks of the Perfume River they weren't surprised. Just another military SNAFU: Situation Normal, All Fucked Up.

"We're not supposed to be here," Second Lieutenant Robert Samuels argued with the swift boat captain. "We're supposed to go to Long Bai."

The captain shook his head. "Sorry, Lieutenant. My orders say I'm supposed to drop you boys here."

"I believe you, but I'm telling you it's a mistake," Samuels continued. "We just got done with a Lurp north of DaNang and we're supposed to brief Headquarters in Long Bai."

The grunts in the bush called long range reconnaissance patrols (LRRP) "lurps."

"And I believe you," the captain said. "All I'm saying is that the orders I have tell me to drop you at Hue. I'm sure it's just a paperwork fuckup. They'll probably have it fixed by tomorrow and I'll be back here to pick you guys up with a freshly cut set of orders."

"Then why can't you just take us now?"

The captain sighed. "Look, Lieutenant, I'm really sorry about this. But I'm not going against what my orders say. I got jammed up doing that before and I don't want to get my tit in a ringer again. OK?"

It was the lieutenant's turn to sigh.

"Yeah, I understand. Sorry for getting pissy."

The captain waved him off. "Forget about it. Just get your men off my fucking boat." He smiled.

Five minutes later the men of Bravo platoon watched the swift boat speed off kicking up a frothy wake as it maneuvered downstream. A minute after that it was nothing more than a memory.

"Now what, LT?" Sergeant John Carter asked.

"Fuck if I know," Lieutenant Samuels muttered. "Goddamn Army."

Carter laughed. He fished a cigarette from a crumpled pack and held it out to Samuels.

"Thanks."

After a few contemplative puffs the Sergeant spoke. "This isn't so bad. I hear Hue has good beer."

Samuels cast a sideways glance at Carter and then snorted. "Always looking on the bright side, Johnny."

"That's why they call me 'Brightside Johnny,'" Carter replied, grinning. "It even says that on my dog tags."

"You're incorrigible."

Carter took another puff. "That's better than being an asshole, I guess."

"Well, you're one of those too," Samuels replied with a smirk.

The troopers sat propped against the bullet-riddled walls of the Citadel, a crumbling structure built by the French during their time in Vietnam. Only then it had been Indo-China. During the Tet Offensive in 1968, Hue had been overrun by the North Vietnamese Army who ransacked the city, killing, raping, and maiming thousands of innocent civilians. After weeks of bloody street battles and house-to-house fighting the Marines eventually retook the city, but it was too late. The once bustling cultural center of South Vietnam had been reduced to ashes.

But now, it was making a comeback. Some of the buildings had been repaired and native foliage replanted and landscaped. There were even a handful of new restaurants and bars, most of which catered to the American GIs' thirst for cheap beer and women.

"I had a buddy who was here in '68 during Tet," Carter said absently. He removed his steel pot and ran a hand through his sweaty mop of dark hair. "He told me the commies went on a killing spree. They found mass graves everywhere. Old men, women, children."

"Yeah, I heard about that too," Samuels replied. "That's fucked up."

"Very poetic, LT," Carter chided his superior. "Did you learn that kind of language working on your master's in English literature at Ohio State?"

Before getting drafted and attending Officer Candidate School, Samuels had been putting the finishing touches on his doctorate in English literature at Ohio State University. The Army had no use for English lit majors so they trained him how to fire an M-16, arm a claymore mine, toss hand grenades, lob mortars into enemy foxholes, and fix a bayonet to the end of his rifle. Basically, how best to kill other men. Then, they gave him two shiny gold bars for his collars and shipped him off to Vietnam to lead men into battle who weren't much younger than he. He wanted to tell the Army that he didn't know shit about leading men into battle, but he could dissect a Shakespearean drama like a surgeon. The dialogue in his head went something like this:

Uncle Sam: "So, Lieutenant Samuels, I understand you know a lot about Shakespeare."

Him: "Yes, sir."

Uncle Sam: "And you were hoping to use this expertise in the Army. Maybe stay Stateside and teach Shakespeare to the troops? Put on a couple plays. That kind of stuff."

Him: "That would be great, sir."

Uncle Sam: "Well, you're in luck. We are in dire need of PhDs in English literature in the Army. Here's the deal: we'll give you an M-16, all the ammunition you can fire, and a bunch of nineteen-year-old kids to spread freedom and democracy throughout Southeast Asia. You can even tell the Vietnamese all about Shakespeare and put on plays in your down time. Deal?"

Him:"Sounds great, sir. Thanks."

The Lieutenant took off his helmet. "Yeah, that's how Shakespeare wrote all his stuff before they edited all the profanity out. *'Alas, poor fucking Yorick. I knew the bastard well.'*"

After a full minute their laughing fit subsided.

"Where did Stinson and Miller go?" Samuels asked.

Carter stood and ground the cigarette butt into the ground with his heel. "They said something about a supply run. You know what that means."

"Women?"

Carter shook his head. "Beer. They both stay away from the ladies. Miller is married, and faithful, believe it or not, and Stinson says he has no intention of catching any creepy crawlies over here."

"Smart. I've heard some nasty things about these women. Hiding razor blades in their...you know...hoo-has." He pointed to his crotch.

"Is that how Shakespeare would describe a vagina?"

The lieutenant laughed again. "No, he'd probably say something like *'pungent, pulsating, meat garden.'*"

"That's nasty," Carter said, his face screwed into a grimacing smirk.

Samuels finished his cigarette and tossed the spent remains aside. He stood, retrieved his rucksack from the dusty ground and slipped the straps over his shoulders. "I suppose we should saddle up and find Chickenman and Miller. See if they had any luck with those supplies."

"Roger that," Carter said, donning his gear. "We could hole up for the night in one of those bombed-out buildings."

"Good idea. Let's make it one of those small ones over there." Samuels pointed to a cluster of blackened shacks that looked like piles of stacked toothpicks. "I don't feel like clearing and securing one of those big buildings."

"You're the boss."

• • •

They found Chickenman and Miller two hundred yards upstream behind one of the local bars on the Perfume River. Calling it a bar was kind; a shed that served warm beer was more accurate.

Miller saw them first. "Hey, Sarge, LT, we're in luck. They've got beer."

Samuels and Carter stopped next to a large steel drum. A bulbous plume of acrid black smoke curled out of the barrel.

"Nice work, guys," Samuels replied. The breeze shifted, pushing fingers of smoke into his face. He coughed, sputtered, and moved out of the way. "What do they have? Budweiser? Heineken? Miller?"

Chickenman and Miller looked at each other and laughed.

"Good one, sir," Chickenman said. "In case you've forgotten we're in Vietnam, not St. Louis."

"So, no Budweiser?"

Miller smirked and shook his head. "Sorry, sir. Only the local brew: *Sukmai Wang*."

Carter looked at the lieutenant and then back at Miller. "You've got to be shitting me. *Sukmai Wang?*"

"Sarge, I'm telling you the God's honest truth," Miller said. "That's what it's called. I'm not making it up. I guess it means 'fermented barley drink,' or something like that."

"Well, I guess it's better than nothing," Samuels muttered. "OK, let's grab a few. We'll at least have something to wash down the C rats with."

C rats were C rations, prepackaged and canned meats, fruit and vegetables; quivering, gelatinous mush that vaguely resembled food. The consensus among the men was that the canned spaghetti wasn't too bad. Canned beef, however, left much to be desired. The lieutenant said he thought it tasted like a regurgitated hamburger.

Carter was about to respond but stopped short. Something wasn't right. Too quiet all of a sudden. A damp chill trickled down his spine and his combat sense tingled. Since arriving in The 'Nam almost a year earlier he'd learned to follow his instincts. If something didn't feel right, no matter how right it appeared on the surface, he listened. Out here, death came swiftly and without warning. If you didn't learn to notice all the subtle cues you were a goner.

Then all hell broke loose.

7

The Men in the Black Pajamas

The men in the black pajamas came out of nowhere. Dozens of them, pouring out of every charred crevice like water through a breached levee.

"Ambush!" John Carter screamed.

Instinctively, each man dove to the ground and sought cover. An instant later the air boiled with the deafening rattle of machine-gun fire, mortars and exploding grenades. Civilians dissolved from sight, leaving isolated pods of American servicemen scrambling for safety near the Citadel. Carter watched two unarmed soldiers freeze in front of a deuce and a half thirty yards north of his position. No guns, no rucksacks, no helmets. Nothing but green combat pants, T-shirts, and their soft caps. Probably company clerks out for a stroll looking for *boom-boom* or *sucky-sucky*.

"Get down!" he screamed at them, but they remained rooted to the ground like statues. "Goddammit, get..."

His words were swallowed by a crushing explosion. He winced and pressed his face to the dusty ground, holding his helmet tightly over his head. A shower of shrapnel and debris rained down on him, plinking off his steel pot like sheets of rain on a tin roof.

He moved quickly after that. He'd seen this before. Bao Dai, three months earlier. Charlie walked artillery and mortar rounds across their perimeter, looking for any American who didn't have the sense to move after the first salvo. Two FNGs fresh from the World bought it that day, too green to know that the piercing shriek they heard meant incoming death.

Carter took cover behind a shattered wall and peeked around the side. The frozen soldiers were mostly gone. What was left of them painted the ground or hung wetly from the overhead palms like moss.

"Sarge! Sarge! We're pulling back." It was Chickenman, tugging on Carter's shoulder, pulling him away from the concrete barrier.

Carter quickly glanced around him; Charlie seemed to be everywhere. "Where are we supposed to pull back to?" he screamed over the deafening roar of the ambush.

Chickenman pointed to a jagged hole blown in the outer wall of the Citadel fifty feet away. On the other side, crouched around the corner firing their M-16s, were Miller and the lieutenant, laying down a blanket of cover fire for a cluster of Marines scrambling from one sandbag-encircled bomb crater to another twenty feet away. As the jarheads tumbled headlong into their new shelter, the crater they had just vacated erupted under a withering barrage of mortar fire, kicking a mushroom cloud of earth and fire thirty feet in the air.

Carter pulled Stinson to the ground. "You make a break for it and I'll cover you," he yelled. "Once you're safe inside with the LT and Miller, you all do the same for me and I'll join you."

Chickenman nodded. Without hesitation he gripped his rifle and tore off across a wide-open no-man's-land, firing wildly as he ran. He could feel the rounds whizzing past him, the air alive with an electric charge and hiss. It was the longest fifty feet of his life. Everything around him seemed to be running in slow motion. The bullets, mortars, and even him. His legs felt heavy, leaden, but he didn't stop. He knew that doing so meant certain death. He at least had a chance if he kept moving. Moving targets were a lot harder to hit.

After what seemed like an eternity, he made it, plunging into the gaping hole in the Citadel's wall, narrowly missing the LT and Miller, landing in a tangled heap.

"You OK?" Miller bent down and dragged his companion off to the side while Samuels continued to provide suppressing fire.

Chickenman sat up and quickly examined himself. He'd seen men hit before and they kept on fighting. Sometimes, the mind was slow in telling the body that it was dead.

"Yeah, no holes," Stinson replied. "Not missing any parts either."

"You're one lucky son of a bitch," Miller said. "I thought for sure you were a goner there. That one mortar round landed about five feet from you."

"Really? Everything was a blur. I knew you guys would keep pouring on the fire, so I just ran." He grabbed his rifle and crouched down. "We need to get Carter over here, now," he continued. "Before Charlie gets a fix on his position. They were hitting that wall pretty hard."

Carter watched anxiously as his comrades twenty feet away scrambled into position and began pouring rounds at two recently established enemy positions behind a cluster of giant palm trees. He was going to count to three and then make a dash for the Citadel.

One. Two...

He jumped up and began moving, hunched over in a modified combat run. After two steps he realized something was terribly wrong. His legs stopped working. He fell to the ground in a heap, rolling and tumbling well short of the relative security behind the Citadel wall. The pain came in searing waves an instant later. He choked back on the nausea. No time for that. He'd deal with it later if he made it out of here alive.

"Sarge is hit!" Chickenman screamed from inside the Citadel.

Another series of explosions, closer to them this time. Charlie finally had a fix on their position, Samuels thought. If they stayed here much longer they'd be dead. Carter too if he wasn't already.

"Cover me," Chickenman yelled over the chaos. "I'm gonna get the Sarge."

"Stinson, wait..."

But the corporal was gone before Samuels could hold him back. He expected no less. The kid might have been slight in stature, but he had cojones the size of basketballs.

"Cover him, Miller," Samuels bellowed.

Halfway there, things went from bad to worse.

• • •

John Carter watched everything through a haze of gunfire, pain, and fear. He saw Stinson bolt from behind the shattered Citadel wall and knew he was coming for him. Part of him thanked God; the other part cursed the kid for being so reckless.

"Go back," he screamed, but his words were swallowed by a fresh barrage of grenade and mortar fire, closer this time.

Carter knew that even if he had heard, Stinson would have kept coming. He'd done this many times before. They all had. Not out of some gung ho, John Wayne sense of duty to God and country. That was Hollywood bullshit. You did it for your buddies. That's how it was out here in the field. That's what it meant to be a grunt. You weren't fighting for some lofty political or social ideology. You fought for the man next to you. You risked your life for a wounded buddy because he would do the same for you. Out here, in the bush, all you had was each other. Fighting for freedom and democracy was an illusion, something they brainwashed you with growing up. Freedom and democracy didn't exist in the bush. All that existed was the man next to you. And the one next to him, on down the line, ad infinitum.

As he lay there wounded, bleeding out, John Carter gave up. He'd never done that before in the bush, never thought about doing it. But, maybe this was it. Maybe his number was finally up. He closed his eyes and resigned himself to the fact that he was going to die. A sense of peace washed over him like warm bathwater. *It's not that bad*, he thought. *Death.*

Floating. He felt like he was floating, high above the chaos below. Then, something brought him back. Someone grabbed him. They were pulling him away from the madness. Sheets of pain shocked him back to reality and he bit his lip.

"Thought you were dead, buddy." It was Chickenman, crouched low, pulling Carter over his back. "Hang on, Sarge."

With Carter on his back Stinson began moving back toward the Citadel fifty feet away. He'd trudged ten feet when the first two rounds slammed into him, knocking him to the ground.

"Fuck, Stinson's hit!" Miller screamed to Samuels.

"Goddammit! Keep that suppressing fire coming."

Samuels pulled a grenade from his waist, yanked the pin and tossed it in the direction of two VC fifteen yards away. Four seconds later they were engulfed in a roiling fireball.

Come on, Chickenman, Samuels thought as he dropped an empty magazine from his smoking rifle and slapped in a new one. *Come on...*

Carter rolled off Stinson's back and into a shallow ditch lined with a slurry of mud and raw sewage. The stench pulled him further back to reality. He gagged, held his breath and glanced over the lip of the depression. Stinson rolled over him, injured, bleeding from a thread of gunshot wounds stitched into his belly.

"You OK, Sarge?" Chickenman's words came out in slow, labored breaths. Carter knew the kid's wounds were bad; worse than his.

"Yeah, I'm good, thanks to you," Carter replied. "How you holding up?"

"Never better," Stinson snorted and then doubled over holding his abdomen.

Carter was about to reply when something rolled into the muddy ditch. Oblong with grooved edges.

"This is it, Sarge," Stinson said. "It's been an honor serving with you guys."

With that, the Chickenman closed his eyes and rolled atop the grenade. He was nineteen years old and forty days and a wake-up short of returning to the World.

8

A Cosmic Kind of Funny

"That's some story." Chuck's words came out slowly, almost in a reverent whisper.

"Yeah, it sure is," Jeff replied. "My dad didn't talk about what happened over there for a long time. When I was really young he just drank a lot. He wasn't abusive or anything like that—just a quiet drunk. Then, he decided to give up drinking. After that he started talking about Vietnam more. I think it helped him come to grips with what happened. Then, I enlisted. I think that made him talk about it even more. It's like he wanted to pass on any advice that would help keep me alive."

"Makes sense. What happened to your dad after that?" Chuck asked.

"He got shipped back home," Jeff answered. "He was hurt pretty bad that last time in Hue. He told me the grunts called it a 'million dollar wound.'"

"Why's that?"

Jeff swatted away a fly that buzzed his ear. The fly returned an instant later only to be sandwiched between the ex-Marine's gloved hands. He wiped the insect's remains on the wooden floor of the truck and removed his gloves.

"Because it was bad enough to get you sent home, but not so bad that it would do any permanent damage."

Chuck nodded. "Did you ever get one of those in Iraq?"

Jeff shook his head slowly. "Nope. Saw plenty of other guys get 'em. Plenty of them get blown to bits or shot too. But I made it out of there intact. Physically, at least."

"You know what's funny?" Jeff continued after a short pause.

"What?"

Jeff stood and shook sleep needles from legs. "If it wasn't for Tommy Stinson, the Chickenman, I wouldn't be here today."

"Yeah, that is funny," Chuck replied. "Not in a ha-ha way. More in a cosmic kind of way. It makes you think about how none of us live in a vacuum. How we're all kind of connected in some way to each other."

Jeff nodded. "That's deep. Especially for a mover. But, yeah, I guess you're right. If it wasn't for Stinson throwing himself on that grenade my dad would have never made it back from Vietnam and I would have never been born. And if it wasn't for my dad giving me Stinson's dog tag, I probably wouldn't have made it home from Iraq."

Chuck looked puzzled. "What do you mean?"

Jeff reached around his neck and pulled something out from beneath his shirt: two dog tags with a jagged hole punched through the center of both.

"I wore Chickenman's dog tags with mine when I was in Iraq," he explained. "For good luck. One day, a sniper nailed me in Baquba. He must have been aiming center mass 'cause the round hit me right in the heart. Right where the dog tags were hanging. The round went through all of them, but it was just enough to redirect the round down my chest. The only thing that happened to me was this."

He lifted his shirt. Chuck saw a jagged white scar, twelve inches long, crisscrossing from Jeff's chest down past his stomach.

"The round traveled just below my skin," Jeff continued, "and exited without doing any damage at all. Only this scar."

Chuck whistled. "Man. Some guy you never even met saved your ass twice."

Jeff nodded in agreement. "Makes you think, doesn't it?" He paused, adrift in some random thought, lost in the zone, again. "It really makes you think...."

Las Cruces

9

Tony Sanchez and the Lost City of Urrao

Tony Sanchez was daydreaming again, gazing out the classroom window at the Organ Mountains when the A-1 moving truck from Colorado rolled to a stop at El Paseo Road and then turned left. He wondered where the truck was headed. Was someone moving into Las Cruces, or far away from it? Hopefully far away. Maybe somewhere cool like Los Angeles or New York. He'd never been to either place. Never been out of New Mexico, actually. The farthest he'd ever traveled from Las Cruces was to Santa Fe when he was four. At least that's what his mother told him. He didn't remember going there.

As the truck rolled out of sight the ten-year-old wished he was out there, in the mountains, maybe on horseback with the sun beating down on him hard, toughening his skin. He'd be searching for gold and lost mines and buried Spanish treasure. It was out there, after all. He'd heard the stories and even checked out books from the school library about it. The lost city of Urrao and its gold-paved streets. Or the Gray Ghost mine, abandoned long ago after a cave-in. Supposedly, there was still a lot of gold there, but no one knew the old mine's exact location. Maybe he'd find it. Maybe this was finally his lucky day. He could see the headline in the paper: *Ten-year-old finds Gray Ghost mine; buys mom new house.* His picture would be under the headline too. He'd given a lot of thought to what he'd wear in the photo. His nicest jeans, the ones with the fewest holes, and his black *Star Wars* T-shirt, the one with Darth Vader and Luke Skywalker fighting each other with their light sabers crossed. Either that or his new Mark Sanchez jersey.

The New York Jets one. It wasn't a real football jersey though; his mom couldn't afford that. Instead, she'd bought a green T-shirt with white sleeves at the Dollar Mart and stitched "Sanchez" on the back.

After a few more moments of careful deliberation he decided on the *Star Wars* shirt. He didn't want to look poor on the front page of the newspaper. Wearing a homemade football jersey might give others that impression. Even if it was the jersey of a football player with the same last name as his. His favorite football player.

Wouldn't it be great if it turned out Mark Sanchez was really his dad? Since he'd never met his father he supposed it was possible. Or was it? He did some quick math in his head and decided that the quarterback would have been somewhere around eleven or twelve when he was born. Not much older than he was right now. Sadly, Mark Sanchez was probably not his dad.

His mother said that his dad had left when he was still a baby. Even if he wasn't his father, maybe the quarterback would marry his mom anyway and adopt him. Then, he wouldn't have to find the lost Gray Ghost mine. That would still be cool, though. Or, even better, finding the mine *and* having Mark Sanchez as his dad.

"…answer, Tony?"

The sound of his name pulled him back to reality. He looked up at the front of the classroom where Mrs. Mooney stood in front of the chalkboard. He liked Mrs. Mooney. She was nice. Pretty too with her long, brown hair and dark eyes. She always smelled good, like cinnamon and vanilla mixed together.

"What?"

A scornful look crossed her face, but it softened almost immediately. Tony Sanchez was one kid she couldn't stay mad at for very long. He may not have been the best student, but he was a kind boy with a heart of gold. She had to admit he held a special place in her heart. Plus, despite his notorious daydreaming, he tried very hard. Part of her thought he tried hard so as not to disappoint her.

"I was asking you if you had the answer to problem number five," his teacher said.

He glanced down at his desk and then back to the front of the room. Mrs. Mooney told him he shouldn't daydream in class, that he should try harder to focus and concentrate. But he couldn't help it. He tried. He really tried, but sometimes his mind just wandered off to places that made him feel good. Made him feel smart and brave. Just like that guy on *Survivorman*. He was cool, and obviously very smart and brave.

"No, ma'am," he replied softly.

"OK, no problem," she said. "Elizabeth, how about you?"

Tony listened as Elizabeth Bates provided the answer. Fortunately, Mrs. Mooney didn't press the issue with him. She'd probably wait until after class and have another talk with him. She seemed to be doing that more and more lately. He didn't mind though. He liked talking with her. It also kept him from heading home right away. The only things that waited there for him were his mom, whom he loved more than anything, and Gary, her new drunk boyfriend who slapped her around a lot. Him too sometimes.

Someone needs to slap that bastard around, he thought as he redirected his gaze back to the mountains on the far eastern horizon. Someone tough like Survivorman. Or Mark Sanchez.

• • •

"Tony, can I have a word with you?"

He stopped at Mrs. Mooney's desk while the rest of his classmates filtered out of the classroom and down the hallway toward the line of waiting buses out front. He walked to school so he didn't have to worry about missing his bus.

"Yes, Mrs. Mooney."

She smiled sweetly, removed her glasses and leaned back in her chair. "You were daydreaming again when I asked you to answer that question, weren't you?"

He nodded slowly. "Yes, ma'am."

"I thought so," she replied. "I can always tell when you're not with us."

"I'm sorry, Mrs. Mooney. I'll try not to let it happen again."

Another smile, this one deeper and more thoughtful. "I've been thinking about that," she said. "It doesn't seem to make any sense for you to promise something you can't deliver. I'm not saying that to get down on you. I'm just saying that it seems really hard for you to concentrate sometimes. Am I right?"

Tony nodded again. She seemed to be going somewhere with this and it had him intrigued.

"So," she continued, "instead of making promises you can't keep I'd like you to do something else."

Now his interest was really piqued.

"What's that?"

"Before I tell you I'd like for you to share something with me. If you feel comfortable, that is."

"Sure," he said as he shrugged. "I can do that."

She stood and pulled her chair around the desk. "Where did you go today when you were daydreaming in class?"

He wasn't sure where she was going with this. The puzzled look on his face told her as much.

"What I mean by that," she explained after sensing his confusion, "is where did you go in your mind? What were you thinking about?"

Now he understood.

He wanted to tell her everything. About the golden city of Urrao and the lost Gray Ghost mine. About Survivorman, and Mark Sanchez being his stepdad. Before the words came tumbling out he stopped himself. She'd probably think it was all stupid. Probably think *he* was stupid. He didn't need that. Not from her. He got enough of that at home from Gary.

"I don't know," he said. "Just thinking about stuff."

"What kind of stuff?" she prodded gently. "No matter what you tell me I promise I won't think it's dumb. You can tell me anything."

That was all he needed to hear. Everything came out in a rush of words. Urrao. The Gray Ghost. Mark Sanchez. Survivorman. Even a few other things that he'd forgotten about. When he was finished he leaned back and smiled.

"Wow, I had no idea," Mrs. Mooney said. She folded her hands in her lap and nodded thoughtfully. "That's quite an imagination you have."

""I guess," Tony shrugged.

"Well, I really appreciate you sharing all that with me. Sometimes it's hard to share what we're feeling or thinking about. Even for adults."

"You don't think I'm stupid for thinking that stuff."

She laughed. "Of course not. I think just the opposite, in fact. You're very smart, and have a very active imagination. That makes you special."

He blushed and allowed a tight smile to creep across his lips. Truth be told, he couldn't help it. Mrs. Mooney thought he was special! The only other person who'd ever said that about him was his mother, and she didn't even say it that often. She was too busy trying to keep Gary happy. Or Bill before Gary came along. Or Ted before Bill left. It seemed she was always trying to hold onto men who liked drinking too much and hurting her.

"What is it you want me to do?" he asked after regaining his composure. "You said you wanted me to do something."

She nodded. "From now on, whenever you start daydreaming I want you to write about it. Any way you want. You can even make up a story around it. In fact, I got this for you."

She reached beneath a pile of papers on her desk and pulled something out. A book with a black cover.

"It's a journal," she continued, "for you to write about whatever you want. Is that something you'd be willing to do?"

She'd read some of the boy's writing. Tony Sanchez had a knack for crafting wildly imaginative stories. He just needed someone to point him in the right direction. Maybe that someone was her.

He took the leather-bound notebook in his hands. The pebbled surface felt cool beneath his skin. No one had ever asked him to do something like this before. His mother was the only person who had taken an interest in anything he did. Right now she was too busy with Gary to do that.

"Yeah, I can do that," Tony replied. "I actually like writing. My favorite is when Mr. Sawyer wants us to make up stories."

Another warm smile and thoughtful nod. "And he says you're very good at it."

"You've talked with him about what I write?" The concept seemed foreign to him.

"Well, yes," Mrs. Mooney replied. "Mr. Sawyer is a very good teacher. And a friend of mine."

The look on his face was priceless: *You have friends?*

"And, yes, teachers have friends," she said as she laughed, intercepting his thoughts. "I've seen that look before, Tony. I know what kids think: teachers are robots. We don't have families or friends. All we like doing is making kids' lives miserable."

This time he laughed. "I don't think you're a robot. Ms. Carson, though. I think she's a robot."

Mrs. Mooney smiled and leaned in conspiratorially. "You know what, I think she's a robot too," she whispered. "But don't tell anyone I said that."

What if Ms. Carson was really a robot, he thought. Or maybe an alien who'd been sent here to spy on earth and prepare things for an invasion of monsters from outer space. Or to turn kids into slaves for the aliens. That would suck. If that ever happened he'd saddle up a couple horses, grab his mom and some food and guns, and head off into the mountains. It wouldn't be hard to hide out there. And the aliens would never find them. But how long would their food last? They'd probably have to do a lot of hunting.

"You're doing it again, aren't you?"

Mrs. Mooney's words broke his reverie.

"Sorry," he replied sheepishly. "Guess I should write about it, huh?"

She nodded and smiled so warmly that he thought it was going to melt his heart. Melting hearts. That was funny. Kind of like the time in that one Indiana Jones movie when that guy's face melted.

10

Gary The Weed

Crap. Gary was home. His tricked out '78 Dodge Charger sat cockeyed next to the trailer, half on the narrow slab of blacktop driveway, half on the meager patch of burnt, thinning grass in front of the double-wide. The car was his pride and joy. Some days he would spend hours drinking beer and washing and waxing her. He called the car "her" a lot, like it was his girlfriend or wife. The fat slob even treated the car better than the woman he claimed to love. Tony had never seen Gary hit the car; his mother wasn't as lucky.

Tony stopped at the bottom of the steps and looked around. A dozen empty beer cans lay scattered around the gleaming Charger and in the small flower bed his mother had abandoned earlier in the summer. A tangle of weeds had taken over, choking out the geraniums and petunias that once bloomed brightly. Gary was kind of like a weed, the boy thought. A worthless, vile weed good for only one thing: strangling beautiful flowers.

Gary The Weed.

He liked that thought and almost laughed out loud. He'd write about that once he was safely locked in his small room. He felt safe there. It was his sanctuary. All he had to do was retreat behind the scarred wooden door and push the lock shut. He'd done that a lot lately, ever since Gary had come along.

Gary The Weed.

He laughed again.

He couldn't remember exactly when The Weed had sprouted up in his life. Probably six months or so ago. Before that, things had been good for a couple of months. Mom had taken a break between boyfriends, something she usually didn't do. Generally, she was on to the next guy before the last one was fully out the door. Tony didn't know why that was. Wasn't he enough for her?

And it wasn't like she was finding decent men. Every one of her boyfriends was a carbon copy of the others: loud, fat, drunk, abusive, and lazy. There was one guy Tony actually liked a couple of years back. What was his name? Ed. Or was it Ted? Something like that. Anyway, he'd been a pretty good guy. He didn't drink much and actually had a job. And he'd never once laid a hand on either of them. His mother dumped Ed or Ted after a couple of months. He didn't get that one. The guy had been nice and decent. He'd even spend time with Tony, playing board games or tossing the football around when Mom was at work. The boy couldn't remember Ed or Ted ever saying one cross word to him. Maybe his mother liked being treated poorly.

OK, deep breath before going inside, then, make a beeline for your room, he thought. Gary's probably drunk. Avoid him, and lock the door. He'd figure dinner out later. Mom's car was gone so she was probably at work. Maybe she left something in the fridge for him. Sometimes she did that.

Sometimes.

The front door swung open before his hand touched the knob.

"Where the fuck have you been?" Gary yelled drunkenly. His massive frame filled the door, all six two, two hundred fifty pounds of him. Only it wasn't a fit two hundred fifty pounds, like an NFL linebacker. His massive belly resembled a side of beef as it hung obscenely over where his waist should have been. He wore only shorts and a pair of grey socks that had once been white. And he smelled awful, worse than usual. A putrid mix of stale alcohol, beefy body odor, and cigarette smoke.

"I…I had to stay after school," Tony stammered.

Partially true. He didn't *have* to stay after school, he wanted to. Mrs. Mooney told him he could stay in her classroom and do some writing while she graded papers if he liked. He jumped at the chance. Anything to avoid going home to Gary The Weed.

He almost laughed again, but caught himself at the last second. That would have been bad. Gary would have seen that as some kind of insult and probably clocked him.

Gary The Weed.

The thought kept coming. He couldn't help it. All he kept seeing was Gary's bloated face atop a body of tangled weeds. Maybe crabgrass. Or poison ivy. Or dandelions. That was the funniest image, actually: Gary's massive melon on top of a thin dandelion stalk, swaying in the breeze. Only it wouldn't be swaying. His head would be plastered to the ground because it was too heavy for the thin stalk to support.

"'Til fucking five o'clock? Who the fuck has to stay after school for two hours?"

Tony wanted to ask the drunk why he cared so much but stopped short. If only he were older, bigger. He'd knock the drunk flat on his ass and drag him out of the trailer. He'd beat Gary The Weed so badly that he'd never want to come back. Then, he'd find a nice guy for his mom. Like Ed or Ted had been. Or maybe Mark Sanchez. He was probably a nice guy.

"I don't know," Tony replied, making sure to keep his eyes down. Gary was like a wild dog in that way. He saw eye contact as a challenge, a reason to attack and fight.

"'*I don't know*'," Gary slurred mockingly. "Well if you don't know, who the fuck does? I sure as hell don't know. Maybe Uncle Sam here knows."

Gary grabbed a wind chime that hung next to the door. It was a wooden cutout of Uncle Sam painted red, white, and blue.

"Hey, Sammy, do you know who has to stay after school for two hours?" He shook the wind chime violently and laughed.

No answer. Only the tinny, metallic jangling of the hollow chimes.

"Looks like old Uncle Sam here doesn't know either. What you got to say for yourself now, boy?"

Nothing, you fat pig, Tony thought to himself. He almost said it out loud but bit his tongue. Now wasn't the time to challenge the drunk. Someday, but not now.

Tony shrugged. He didn't know what else to say. "Can I come in now? I have to pee."

He didn't really have to pee, but thought that might get Gary to move out of the way. He was right.

"Get in here," the drunk snarled menacingly. He pushed the battered screen door open and pulled Tony inside. Then, for no particular reason, he started hitting the boy.

11

Good Morning, Mrs. Mooney

The first thing Catherine Mooney noticed as class started the next morning was Tony Sanchez's empty seat. She wasn't worried at first; still five minutes before the bell rang. Plus, she knew two buses were running late due to an accident on the interstate. Marjorie Johnson, the school secretary, had relayed that message to her earlier in the school office. That would explain the empty seats. But then she remembered that Tony walked to school.

He wasn't typically late. In fact, he was usually the first one seated in her classroom. He didn't miss much school either. Only two days so far this year, and that had been during a particularly bad outbreak of strep throat that had affected both students and staff.

She shuffled through a stack of corrected papers, pulled one from the middle and set it aside. Two minutes before the hour and three of her four missing students trudged through the front door, chatting excitedly. She smiled and said good morning to all of them. Britney Montoya was the only one who smiled back. The other two girls were too busy chatting about who liked who, pierced ears, and some nonsense about the Jonas Brothers. That left Tony Sanchez as the only missing student.

The bell rang and still no Tony.

"Good morning, everyone." She stood and walked over to the chalkboard.

"Good morning, Mrs. Mooney." The collective, sing-song greeting was feeble and less than enthusiastic.

Nothing strange about that, she thought. Just kids being kids.

"Looks like everyone's here today," she said as she checked off the names in her attendance book. "Except for Tony. Did anyone see him this morning?"

Some shaking heads, a few blank stares. Most of the kids just stared off into space.

"OK, well, let's get started, then."

She was about to launch into the details of the Gadsden Purchase when there was a knock on the classroom door. Through the glass she saw the matronly face of Marjorie Johnson, a concerned look stitched across her brow.

"Excuse me for a second," she told her students as she closed the social studies textbook and walked to the door.

"Hi, Cathy, sorry to bother you," Marjorie whispered as she poked her head inside the doorjamb.

"That's OK."

A low murmur began circulating through the room like an electric current. Another common occurrence when something or someone disrupted the organized rhythm of the day.

"Hey, let's keep it down," Mrs. Mooney gently reminded her students. "Start reading chapter nine. We'll be covering that in just a few minutes."

She stepped into the hallway and closed the door shut behind her. "So, what's going on?"

Marjorie shifted uncomfortably and pulled a pink phone memo from her pocket. "Tony Sanchez won't be in today."

A lump formed in Catherine Mooney's throat. Something wasn't right here. She could feel it.

"Why not?" For some reason she feared the answer.

A short pause while Marjorie studied the memo. "He's in Mesilla Valley Hospital. There was some kind of accident last night…"

12

Accident, My Ass

"Accident, my ass," Catherine Mooney muttered between clenched teeth as she navigated the light swells of midafternoon traffic on her way to Mesilla Valley Hospital. She'd managed to control her anger most of the day, losing herself in the various lesson plans: Gadsden Purchase, The Mexican-American War, geometry. But now she was pissed. The whole "accident" thing with Tony Sanchez had set her off. She was almost positive that whatever happened to him was no accident. She didn't know everything about his home life, but she knew enough.

Apparently, his mother's boyfriend liked to drink and had a temper. Mom didn't seem to be the most stable either. Flighty, needy, unreliable. At least that's the impression she'd gotten after meeting with Amy Sanchez at the last parent-teacher conference. Really, that's all she had to go on at this point.

Calm down, she thought. *You don't even know what happened yet.*

She took a few deep breaths and that seemed to help. Maybe it really was an accident. Ten-year-old boys could be reckless and wild. Although, she'd never seen Tony act like that. He was always quiet, pensive, thoughtful. Still, she supposed that even the most demure ten-year-old boy could have his reckless moments.

Still, something in the back of her mind kept repeating the same thing: *Accident, my ass.*

• • •

"He's in room B-3." The nurse at the front desk pointed absently down the hallway with one hand while the other punched a few keys on the computer keyboard.

"Thanks," Catherine Mooney replied.

She found room B-3 at the end of the antiseptic hallway, the door halfway open. A white sheet strung from a track on the ceiling obscured her view into the room. She knocked on the door frame.

"Tony. It's Mrs. Mooney," she whispered.

"Who?" A gruff voice, deep and thorny came from the other side of the sheet. Obviously not Tony's, unless he'd gone through puberty since yesterday.

"Uh...Mrs. Mooney, from school."

A large hand, hairy and misshapen with knobby knuckles shoved the white curtain aside. The man attached to that hand was just as hairy and misshapen, with a gut that bubbled obscenely beneath a stain-splotched wife-beater T-shirt. Next to him stood Tony's mother, small and mousy with stringy blonde hair, high cheekbones, and a fresh black eye. A curt nod and she turned her gaze to the green tiled floor.

"Oh, Tony's teacher," the hairy man leered. He smiled and ran his eyes up and down Mrs. Mooney. "I'm Gary Daniels."

He stuck his hand out. Reluctantly, she took it and immediately regretted her decision. His paw felt rough, sweaty, and he held her hand in his for too long. She pulled away and wiped her hand on her jeans. She didn't care if Gary Daniels took note of that. He was creeping her out already and she'd been in his presence less than a minute.

"Mrs. Mooney?" Tony's voice, small and uncertain, came from behind the curtain.

Catherine stepped around Gary Daniels and Amy Sanchez. "Hey, kiddo," she said as she stepped to the boy's bedside and took his hand in hers. Unlike the hairy oaf, Tony's hand was small, frail. That's when she noticed the soft cast on his left arm, two black eyes and line of fresh stitches above his right eye.

"What are you doing here?" he asked.

"I came to see you," she replied, startled at his appearance. "They said you were in the hospital so I wanted to stop by and see how you were doing."

He tried sitting up but found it difficult. Obviously in pain, she thought.

"Sorry about missing school today," he mumbled.

She chuckled and patted his arm reassuringly. "Don't worry about it, kiddo. Looks like you have a pretty good excuse. I don't think you'll get detention for this."

He smiled feebly but said nothing. Silence settled over the room like a dark shroud. Gary and Tony's mom moved to the other side of the room near a bank of windows. Even though the hairy oaf was behind her, out of sight, she could feel his eyes crawling over her hips and butt. It made her want to gag. What did Amy Sanchez see in him? She wasn't an unattractive woman. Fresh shower and a bit of makeup and she was as pretty as anyone.

"So, what happened?" Mrs. Mooney finally asked, breaking the interminable silence.

Tony's gaze darted nervously at Gary, and then back to his teacher. Something secret lurked behind those dark eyes, Catherine Mooney thought.

"He fell down the steps," Gary quickly interjected. Too quickly, like it had been rehearsed. "Poor kid. I told him not to run in the house, but you know how boys are. Always on the go."

Catherine nodded. "Really? Mobile homes come with steps these days?"

The words slipped out before she could pull them back. She knew Tony lived in *Sagebrush Acres*, a collection of ramshackle trailers a mile from school. To the best of her recollection double-wide trailers didn't have staircases.

"Uh…yeah," Gary stammered, the smug, leering look gone from his face. "The front steps. They're kinda worn out. Little man here couldn't wait to get outside and play with his buddies. Took a header right off the top step. Ouch."

She should have held her tongue but couldn't help it. This wasn't really any of her business. All she had was a *feeling* that something wasn't right in the Sanchez household. She had no proof.

"Is that what really happened, Tony?"

After posing the question her eyes darted back to the windows meeting Gary Daniels' gaze head-on. The look in his eyes told her he didn't like that. She got the distinct impression that the oaf wasn't used to being challenged.

"Yeah, that's what really happened," Gary answered, his tone menacing and icy.

Catherine Mooney didn't back down. "I'm sorry," she said calmly, "I was asking Tony."

What are you doing? The voice in the back of her mind queried. *This is none of your business. Stay out of it. You're only going to make things worse.* Then, another voice chimed in, stronger, more insistent. *Fuck it. This guy's a dirtbag.*

She chose to listen to the profane voice.

"Is that what happened, Tony?" she repeated, pressing the point.

After a couple of nervous glances in Gary's direction Tony nodded uncertainly. "Yeah."

Actually, she expected this. She didn't think the boy would come out and say, *No, Mrs. Mooney, I didn't fall down the front steps. Gary beat the shit out of me.* Still, she was glad she pressed the issue. If nothing else, it put the dirtbag on alert that someone was watching out for Tony. It may not have been the person who should have been doing that—his mother—but someone had the boy's back. And Catherine Mooney was determined not to let Tony Sanchez down.

13

Gary The Weed Part II

For two days the same obsessive phrase ran through his booze-addled brain on a continuous loop: *the fucking bitch!*

Mooney. The kid's teacher. She'd shown up at the hospital asking questions like she was fucking Perry Mason or something. Nosy bitch. None of it was any of her business. She seemed like one of those uppity cunts who didn't know the meaning of MYOFB: Mind Your Own Fucking Business!

Despite all that, she looked good. Tight ass, nice tits and the kind of face that would look good covered with his spunk. That's what Gary thought about as he lay jerking off in bed. Mooney's mouth, working him over. Cocksucker-red lips sliding up and down his shaft, all the way down to his balls. He'd make her go deeper too. Grab her by the hair and push it to the back of her throat 'til she gagged on it. 'Til she fucking cried. Then, just as he was about to lose it, he'd pull out of her mouth and shoot his load all over that pretty face of hers.

That final image did it. He exploded in his hand, jerking furiously until it hurt.

The fucking bitch. He'd show her.

14

Captain Crabgrass and the Milkweed Bunch

Two days after his "accident" Tony was glad to be back in school. He still had the black eyes, but the swelling had gone down some. The cut above his eye still stung a little and his cracked forearm ached, but he was glad to be here. It was a million times better than being at home with that fat piece of crap Gary.

Two days away from school, stuck in the hospital bed with his mom and Gary visiting about two hours total, had given him a lot of time to write. During his stay he'd filled nearly half his new journal with all sorts of stuff. Short stories, a couple of characters he'd made up, and a bunch of random doodles that covered nearly every page. He found drawing helped stimulate the creative part of his brain. He'd start by just drawing random shapes and then keep adding to them. Then, he'd examine the sketches and write about what he saw. Most of it was nonsense, but he didn't care. It felt good to create the pictures and his stories.

He'd even done a couple of sketches of Gary as a big-headed dandelion. He liked those drawings so much that he started writing a story about a group of superheroes who were plants or weeds: Captain Crabgrass, Dan. D. Lion, Milkweed Jones, Creeping Charlie, and Sandy Sumac. He called them The Milkweed Bunch.

One of the nurses had been kind enough to set up her laptop for him so he could surf the Net for information on weeds. He learned a lot: where different kinds grow and what they looked like. If they were poisonous or not. The most interesting thing he read, though, was about weed control. And that gave him another idea. One he decided not to write a story about. At least not yet.

• • •

"How are you feeling?"

Mrs. Mooney stopped him after the rest of the kids had left her classroom.

He shrugged. "OK, I guess."

"You know, I was worried about you. I'm glad you're back."

Mrs. Mooney, worried about him? He felt something funny in the pit of his stomach. A warm sensation that made him feel special, cared for. Something he wasn't entirely used to.

"I'm glad to be back too," he replied. "Being in the hospital was kinda boring."

She laughed. "I know what you mean. When I was a teenager I had to have my appendix taken out. I should have been out of the hospital after a couple days, but I had an infection so they kept me there for a week. I was so bored by the time I left I thought I was going to go crazy."

Tony grinned, first trying to picture Mrs. Mooney as a teenager, and then going crazy.

"I felt like that sometimes too," he confessed. "But I got to do a lot of writing." He held up his journal for her to see.

A delighted twinkle danced in her eyes. "Really? That's great, Tony. What have you been writing about?"

He told her all about Captain Crabgrass and The Milkweed Bunch and she laughed.

"I love the names," she said, still smiling. "Very creative."

"You think so?" He seemed surprised.

"Absolutely. Not too many kids your age have that kind of imagination, or the ability to put those ideas into a story. In fact, most adults don't either."

"Well, I've just been doing what you told me to do—write about the things that I think about. It's really not that hard. And I like doing it."

She smiled warmly and leaned back. She'd told herself earlier that she wasn't going to ask Tony any more about the accident. That horse had been beaten to death at the hospital. But now, with him standing in front of her with his black eyes, stitches, and broken arm, she couldn't help herself.

"Hey, remember when I stopped by the hospital to see you the other day?" she said.

Tony nodded.

"Well, I was just really worried about you. I still am. You didn't get hurt running off the front steps, did you?"

Why do you keep doing this? The cautious voice in the back of her mind was back, berating her again for taking such an interest in Tony Sanchez. *Leave well enough alone.*

The other voice, the profane one, chimed in. It always did.

Leave well enough alone? Fuck that. The kid's in trouble.

Tony didn't answer. Not a nod or shake of his head. Only a steely silence that seemed to linger too long. His face changed though. Gone was the relaxed smile and sparkling eyes. Instead, the boy wore a mask of hesitation and fear.

"You don't have to answer, Tony," Mrs. Mooney finally said. "Maybe it's none of my business. I'm sorry for bringing it up again."

"That's OK," Tony replied. "You don't have to be sorry. It really was an accident, just like Gary said."

He didn't like lying to Mrs. Mooney, but if Gary found out he'd told anybody about the beating the next one would be even worse. The fat creep might even kill him.

Unless Captain Crabgrass and The Milkweed Bunch got to him first.

15

Watching the Watcher

He watched her from the woods behind the school. Far enough away that she couldn't see him, but close enough that he could make out her curves and contours. Hips, ass, chest. Things he'd been dreaming about nonstop since first meeting her at the hospital last week. Things that had brought him to orgasm three times daily since then.

It was shortly after that first encounter in the hospital that he decided he wanted her. Wanted to hurt her. Not just because she was a nosy bitch. Sure, that was part of it, but there was more to it than that. He had done all this before and found that he liked it, had a taste for it.

Gary had found this spot behind the school three days earlier after deciding he was going to kill Mrs. Mooney. But just killing her would be a terrible waste. He planned on having a little fun first. And he knew just the place: an abandoned hunting camp in the mountains about an hour from here. It was secluded and private, tucked in a narrow canyon with only one way in and one way out. He figured he could probably keep her there for a week, bound and gagged, before killing and burying her in some nameless hole. God, he couldn't wait. A whole week of forcibly fucking that bitch. Just thinking about it now made him stiffen.

In the fading daylight he reached for the bottle next to him and took a long pull of the only courage he knew. The golden mash burned as it slid down his throat. He wiped his lips on the back of his sleeve and went back to watching the teacher as she slipped behind the wheel of her Honda Civic and pulled out of the school parking lot. Soon he would make his move. Very soon.

• • •

Catherine Mooney's watcher had a watcher of his own. Two dark orbs pressed to the rubber eyeholes of a battered set of camouflage binoculars. Eyes that had watched the drunk with searing intensity every evening for the past three nights. Eyes belonging to someone very intent on making sure no harm came the teacher's way. Catherine Mooney didn't deserve becoming the object of Gary Daniels' anger and smoldering obsession. She was a good person, one who cared about others and would go out of her way to help someone in need. Just like she'd done for Tony Sanchez.

The journal she'd given him had been more than just a book in which to write stories and doodle. The significance of that leather-bound tome ran much deeper than that. To him, it was perhaps the nicest thing that anyone had ever given him. Better than the newest electronic gadget, video game, or shiny new bike. Not that he had any of that stuff anyway. In the annals of gift giving it was, on its face, relatively unremarkable. But the boy loved it, not because it was something expensive or extravagant, but because it came from her heart. It showed she cared about him. And that was more than anyone else in the orbit of his life had ever done for him.

• • •

Something rustled in the dense scrub behind him and his heart jumped. Out here it could be anything. Snakes. Prairie dogs. Maybe even a coyote. More brittle rustling, like the rattling of dry bones, and the coarse snapping of twigs, closer this time. Then, without warning, the threat bolted from the brush in a smear of fur.

He breathed a sigh of relief once the rabbit was out of sight. The mission had not been compromised. The thought made him chuckle. That was how real spies spoke. *Mission compromised. Target acquired. Target neutralized.* During his stay in the hospital he'd also Googled "spies" and learned about how they worked and spoke. That had been interesting too. Maybe not as useful as what he learned about weed control and herbicides, but still pretty cool.

After a few moments his heart stopped racing and he returned to the binoculars. The drunk was still there, seated atop a broad tree stump and still nursing his bottle. This was it, the last night of watching Gary. After tomorrow that piece of crap would never bother anyone again. Captain Crabgrass and The Milkweed Bunch would see to that.

• • •

16

The Last Roundup

Man's body found behind school
By Andrea Guerrero

LAS CRUCES—A man's body was found yesterday morning behind Mesilla Park Elementary School. Authorities identified the man as Gary Daniels, 35, of Las Cruces. According to reports, police found a half-empty whiskey bottle next to Daniels, along with what appeared to be a "rape kit" containing rope, duct tape and rubber gloves. Testing revealed the bottle contained the herbicide Roundup mixed with whiskey. "At this point foul play is not suspected in this death," said Sgt. Bill Cummings, spokesperson for the Las Cruces Police Department. "By all accounts, it appears to be a bizarre suicide."

Seattle

16

Mr. Yuck

What a horrible way to die, Charlotte Taylor thought as she finished scanning the news article. The story had popped up on the *Las Cruces Sun-News* Web site, one of the media outlets she found herself randomly surfing from time to time. She wasn't sure why she clicked on the story in the first place. Nothing remarkable about it, other than the fact that the guy's body had been found behind a school. Oh, and that he'd apparently offed himself by ingesting Roundup.

Ouch.

She'd done that once as a kid. Not Roundup but some household cleaning product. The details were a bit fuzzy now, except for the nasty taste and burning sensation as whatever it was—Comet or 409—ate its way down her throat. And that wasn't even the worst part.

At the emergency room they pumped her stomach. She could remember crying hysterically and thrashing about as her parents tried holding her down. The doctor had been as gentle as he could, but it didn't matter. There was no real way to repeatedly force a plastic suction tube down someone's throat into their stomach and *gently* suck the poison out.

At least she'd learned her lesson. For the remainder of her childhood years she steered clear of the cabinet under the sink with the green "Mr. Yuck" sticker plastered to the front. She even remembered the jingle: *Mr. Yuck is mean. Mr. Yuck is green.* Her parents had gotten the stickers after the whole stomach pumping incident. Too bad they hadn't thought about that before. Maybe she would have stayed out of there.

Or maybe not. She'd been a curious child, after all, always asking *why* or *how. Why is the sky blue? How does a steam engine work? Why are there pygmies?* And on and on and on.

Her parents had lovingly nicknamed her the *Questionator*, eventually shortening the moniker to simply *Q.* That's what they still called her. Her brother too. Not her husband though. He had other pet names for her, most of them X-rated.

The very thought of Mark brought a smile to her face. He'd had that effect on her ever since she'd first laid eyes on him at the student center their senior year at UCLA. She'd picked him up, although he still maintained that it was he who'd done the picking up. Either way, they clicked instantly and the chemistry was undeniable. Movies, dinner, long walks, marathon phone calls. They were inseparable. By the end of the semester she knew she loved him. He said the same.

After graduation he landed a well-paying job with Bullseye Corporation in Seattle. They tried the long distance thing but the time spent apart was interminable. She relocated three months later, piling everything she owned in the back of the "Om," a 1990 Dodge Omni with the "n" and "i" missing from the rear nameplate.

Five weeks after that they flew to Las Vegas and got married by Elvis in a cheesy faux chapel on the north end of the Strip. They both agreed it was the craziest thing they'd ever done. They also agreed it would be a great story to tell the grandkids someday.

That was three years ago and the honeymoon hadn't stopped. She'd heard from tons of other couples that sometimes marriage wasn't easy. That it took a lot of hard work and dedication. So far, their marriage had been effortless. Mark was as close to perfect as was humanly possible: open, committed and not afraid to talk about things. Unlike so many of the men whose paths had crossed hers during her dating years. She couldn't even remember the last time they'd had a fight. Maybe last year at his company's holiday party after she thought a female coworker had paid a little too much attention to Mark. And even that hadn't been much of a fight. Ten minutes of hurt feelings and miscommunication, followed by two hours of making up in the sudsy confines of their bubble-loaded oversize tub.

The thought of that night brought another smile to her face. Suddenly, she couldn't wait to get home.

• • •

The interstate was backed up like a clogged drain. Choosing this route had been a titanic mistake. She'd checked the traffic report before leaving the office and saw that a jackknifed semi on her usual way home had everything at a standstill. It was worse here. She'd forgotten about the construction on the University Bridge. Resurfacing and widening the lanes had traffic filtered down to one narrow sliver of stripped, grooved pavement in either direction with no room to spare. The only thing that separated her from Portage Bay eighty feet below was a train of concrete barriers lined up to her right.

Stupid, she thought. She wanted to get home as quickly as possible. All she could think about was another bubble bath tonight with Mark, warm and wet, just like she was starting to feel. Plus, she had something else to share with him. A surprise. Something they had been talking about for the past year or so.

She reached for the plastic Ziploc bag on the passenger seat. If she was reading the test correctly the little pink plus symbol told her their lives were about to change dramatically. Still, she couldn't believe it. Pregnant? She was going to be a mom and Mark, a dad. *Mom and Dad*. The idea seemed foreign to her. She supposed it would take some time to get used to. That was OK. They had the rest of their lives to do that.

Brake lights flashed in front of her again, just like they'd been doing intermittently for the past quarter mile. Bored with the radio she plugged her earpiece in and punched in her brother's number on her cell phone. Two years her senior, Eddie was living the life of a happy bachelor in Tampa. He worked for FDOT as a civil engineer fixing old roads and building new ones. All this construction on the University Bridge would be right up his vocational alley. She wondered if he'd ever consider moving here. She missed him and had a friend at work who she'd love to set him up with. Sweet, funny, and terribly attractive, Tina Meyer would be perfect for Eddie. With his skills and background, he'd have no trouble finding a job here either. All she had to do was get him to give up the tropical warmth of south Florida for the rainforests of Seattle. Not an easy sell.

Five rings and his voice mail clicked in. *"Hey, it's Eddie. You know the drill."*

"Hi, Eddie, it's me. Just called to say hi and see how you're doing. Call me when you get a chance. Hey! What the hell…"

Tampa

17

Sinkholes and Skeletons

A continent away Eddie Clark felt the cell phone vibrating in his pocket but he couldn't get to it. He was stuck working overtime at the scene of a massive sinkhole that had opened next to Tatum Road. As a result, a five-acre pond nearby collapsed, pushing all of the water into the surrounding wetlands and onto Tatum Road. But that wasn't the worst of it. Mired to the mucky bottom of the pond bed was the rusted shell of a 1970 Chevy Impala. No big deal, right? It wasn't an issue until two surveyors waded into the muck and looked in the car. Sinkholes in Florida weren't unusual; sinkholes that drained ponds that contained submerged cars with human skeletons in the back seat were.

"Don't touch a thing," Eddie cautioned his crew. "Not until the police tell us we can."

"This is going to put things even more behind schedule," Marty Vance, one of the surveyors who found the skeletons, said. "Who knows how long it's going to be before they do their thing here."

Eddie shrugged. He removed his yellow hard hat and ran a hand through his tangled mop of matted-down hair. "So be it. This is way beyond fixing a road now."

The efficiency of the Tampa Police Department surprised them all. Within three hours they had pulled the Impala from the mud and conducted a grid search for any more evidence. By six the car with the skeletons was on the back of a flatbed tow truck headed for the forensics garage downtown. An hour after that Eddie's crew broke for the day, grateful to finally escape the unrelenting heat.

"It's not the heat, it's the humidity," someone told him when he first moved down here. And they were right. He'd never felt humidity like this before. It was oppressive and heavy, like a wet shroud.

Now, after two years, he was used to it. Since half of his work time was spent outdoors he had no choice. Besides, he liked it here. What more could a single, twenty-eight-year-old guy ask for? Good-paying job, apartment near the ocean, and plenty of eligible, scantily clad females lining the beaches. Row upon firm row of slender legs, tight butts, and fake breasts. Life was good.

• • •

At Morgan and Bell he stopped for a red light. Jack in the Box beckoned to him from the northeast corner. The siren song was too great for him to resist. He turned right and eased into the drive-through. Two minutes later he left with a paper sack containing more than two thousand calories of fat and grease. Perfect bachelor fare.

As he eased into traffic he remembered the cell phone in his pocket. Two new messages. One from his friend Dallas Harper and the other from Charlotte.

"Hi, Eddie, it's me. Just called to say hi and see how you're doing. Call me when you get a chance." A short, uncertain pause, and then, *"Hey! What the hell..."*

The line went dead after that. Probably a bad connection. He'd call her back once he got home. After consuming the artery-clogging contents of the Jack in the Box bag in front of the TV, of course.

He spread the contents of the bag atop a TV tray: sirloin cheeseburger, large fries, and an order of jalapeño poppers. At least he had the four food groups covered. Or was it five? Whatever. It tasted good. Screw the five food groups.

He turned on the flat panel television and began absently flipping through channels. More bombings in Iraq on CNN, a bridge collapse on Fox News, and Keith Olbermann screeching incoherently on MSNBC. Then he found what he was really looking for: ESPN.

The burger was gone in five bites and the fries five minutes later. He leaned back on the couch and contemplated making a move for the jalapeno poppers but stopped short. Too full. He'd save them for later. Maybe breakfast.

He muted the TV volume, reached for his cell phone and punched in Charlotte's number. Voice mail. He left her a message and went back to the TV. ESPN had gone to commercial so he resumed flipping channels. *Diners, Drive-ins and Dives* on Food Network, something about the Mafia on NatGeo, *Ghost Hunters* on Syfy. He decided to go back to CNN and catch up on the news of the day. Maybe they'd have something on the sinkhole. The images that greeted him were of the bridge collapse he'd flipped past earlier. It looked pretty bad. He turned up the volume.

"...people are confirmed dead," the anchor reported. He shuffled through a stack of papers and held one up, examining it closely. "Actually, we've just had an update on the number of casualties. Authorities have now confirmed fifteen dead and eleven still missing. In case you've just joined us we are covering a terrible bridge collapse in Seattle. The University Avenue Bridge simply fell apart with dozens of cars on the bridge at the time."

Eddie almost flipped back to ESPN but he stopped. *Seattle?* Charlotte lived there. A blooming sense of unease began gnawing at him. Her voice mail from earlier had ended abruptly. Could she have been on the bridge? It seemed unlikely. What were the odds of being on that bridge at the exact moment of its collapse? Pretty slim, actually. More than likely it was just a bad connection. What probably happened was that the cell phone provider had been overwhelmed with calls coming out of Seattle. People calling their loved ones telling them they were OK.

Despite trying to convince himself that his sister's cutoff phone message was nothing more than a bad connection, the uneasy feeling in the pit of his stomach didn't go away. Then, his cell phone rang.

• • •

"Dude, what's up?" It was Dallas Harper.

"Hey, D," Eddie replied, sitting up on the couch, momentarily forgetting Seattle. "Not much. Just got done eating."

"Late dinner, huh?"

"Yeah. I had to work late today. Sinkhole opened up over by Tatum."

"Hey, I saw that on the news earlier," Dallas said. "Thing was huge. They said something about a car being found with a couple of bodies in the back seat. You were out there?"

"Yup. It was weird too. All the water drained out of this big pond and there was this old Chevy just sitting there. A couple of guys in my crew checked it out and found two skeletons in the back seat. Cops came out after that and towed the car."

Random shuffling from the other end of the line, followed by a muffled thud. "Sorry," Dallas mumbled a few moments later. "Dropped the phone."

Eddie laughed. "Did you trip over a pile of junk on the floor?"

Although older by fifteen years, Dallas had the organizational skills of a college freshman. His sparsely furnished apartment looked more like a sloppy dorm room than the living quarters of a man over forty. Still, Eddie liked him. With Dallas, there was no pretension. He was a slob and proud of it.

"Yeah," he said as he laughed heartily. "I just got a bunch of old *National Geographic* magazines at a garage sale. Tons of them. Probably like two hundred, some of them from the fifties. Still trying to find a place to put them though. Right now they're just piled up on the floor. In fact," more rustling from the other end of the line, "I'm looking at this one right now about a tribe of Pygmies in Africa. There's this one photo where they're all sitting around a fire cooking some kind of dead rodent and they're all naked. And the women have those saggy, torpedo tits that hang down to their belly buttons. Nasty. It's Pygmy porn."

"You need help," Eddie joked. "Sigmund Freud kind of help."

"Freud?" Dallas muttered. "Didn't he have a thing for his mom?"

Eddie scanned his memories for the lecture notes from Psychology 101. Freud. Drug addict. Oedipus Complex. Obsessed with sex. "I don't know," he finally replied. "Probably."

"Hey, how'd things go with that one broad the other night?" Dallas asked. "Stacy. Or was it Tracy?"

"*Broad?* Who are you, part of the Rat Pack? Frank Sinatra? Dean Martin?"

Dallas laughed loudly, only Eddie wasn't sure if it was at him or at the torpedo-titted Pygmy women he was probably still ogling in *National Geographic.*

"OK then. *Chick, filly.* Whatever you call women nowadays."

"And all this time I've been wondering why you're still single."

"Me too. Anyway, how'd that all go with…"

"Stacy," Eddie finished the thought. "Good. She's nice, but…I don't know…I guess I just didn't feel any kind of connection."

"Did you *schtup* her?"

"No, Mr. Sinatra, I did not *schtup* her."

"No wonder you didn't feel any sort of connection," Dallas mumbled almost incoherently. Now he was munching on something.

"I'm not just looking to get laid," Eddie said.

"Blasphemy! Why not?"

Eddie was about to launch into an explanation when his phone beeped. Mark and Charlotte's home number appeared on the caller ID and a sense of relief set in. Charlotte was probably calling to let him know she was OK. The bridge collapse had made world news, after all.

"Hey, sorry, D, I've got another call coming in," he said. "I'll call you tomorrow."

"Cool. Later."

Eddie clicked over and his brother-in-law's voice greeted him, distant and robotic. It sounded like he'd been crying.

18

Dallas Does Tampa

Dallas Harper hung up the phone and returned his attention to the pile of *National Geographic* magazines scattered across the floor. He'd had enough of looking at Pygmies so he reached for one with a photo of a heavily bundled climber trudging up the icy backbone of K2, the world's second-tallest mountain. He flipped through the magazine absently, paying more attention to the photos than the words. It's not that he couldn't read—he had a bachelor's degree in criminology—he simply didn't do it that often. Reading was time consuming and boring, and he was a man of action. At least that's how he saw himself.

After getting kicked out of the police academy in Los Angeles he found himself aimlessly drifting east. A few months in Phoenix working at a car wash. Six months in Houston risking his life on an offshore oil rig. A year scraping burgers off a grill at a greasy spoon in New Orleans. Finally, he landed in Miami, his eastward momentum halted by the Atlantic Ocean. He backtracked a few months later, stopping in Tampa. This time it was the Gulf of Mexico that kept him in place. He liked it so much he decided to stay.

That was twenty years ago.

He still had a hard time believing it had been that long. Time had gotten away from him. Now, he was pushing forty-five (or pulling forty, as he liked to say) with not much to show for it. A moderately successful career as a private investigator, small apartment near downtown, and a 1988 Toyota Celica that sometimes ran. Nothing like Thomas Magnum's set up in Hawaii on *Magnum P.I.* He had the run of an exclusive estate and could take Robin Masters' Lamborghini out whenever he wanted. Provided Higgins didn't get in the way.

Unfortunately for Dallas Harper, his life had not turned out anything like Tom Selleck's character on TV in the 1980s. Still, he had to admit he was happy. He had a roof over his head and a job that paid the bills most of the time. Would he have liked more? Sure, who wouldn't? Bill Gates probably wanted to make more money.

But Dallas' life hadn't been about climbing any corporate ladder or filling his bank account with obscene amounts of cash. In his humble opinion life was about living. It was about sucking each day dry by doing what you wanted to do. The future never particularly bothered him. He'd worry about tomorrow when it became today.

In that way he was different from most of his family and friends. He came from a large family—two brothers and two sisters. He was the youngest, and, in his opinion, the happiest. Not that the others weren't happy or decent people. None of them were drug addicts, criminals, or deadbeats. He got along with all of them; they were just all very different from him.

That was one thing that had always fascinated him. How five people from the same gene pool, raised in the same petri-dish household, could blossom into such different people. His oldest brother, Ted, was a doctor in San Francisco. Next in line was his sister Cat, an attorney for some big law firm in Los Angeles. Todd was the middle child and had chosen a career in environmental activism, running interference for whales being chased by harpoon-spitting Japanese trawlers. Marlene was a lesbian writer who'd actually sold some of her antimale books along the way. Then, there was him.

His path in life had been the one of least resistance. Especially after getting kicked out of the police academy in LA. That whole episode still irked him. How was he supposed to know Chief Braxton's daughter was only sixteen? She looked older.

Anyway, that was all ancient history, now. Part of him was glad he never became a cop. He had friends from the academy he still kept in touch with and many of them had become cynical, withdrawn alcoholics because of the job. Back then all he wanted to do was cruise the streets and chase down bad guys. Like most young people he'd been headstrong and idealistic, thinking that he could actually make a real difference in the world. Maybe change some things. As time went by, however, he came to realize that nobody ever really changes the world. Actually, it worked the other way around: the world changed you.

•   •   •

Somewhere, *Viva Las Vegas* played loudly. In the semidarkness Dallas groped for his cell phone. He'd fallen asleep on the couch with the K2 issue of *National Geographic* tented over his chest. From the battered coffee table in front of the couch Elvis continued crooning about fortunes being won or lost on the roll of a dice.

"Hello." His voice was sandpaper dry and heavy with sleep. In his head he thought he sounded like a croaking bullfrog.

"Mr. Harper?" The voice, feminine with a southern California lilt, was unfamiliar.

"Yeah, speaking." Why was his mouth so dry? It felt pasty, like he'd been out partying the night before. The only thing he had to drink last night was a can of Coke.

"My name is Melanie Treadwell," the woman continued. "I got your name from Reggie Bannister. He said he hired you last year and that you were reliable and discreet."

Dallas sat up on the couch and scratched his head. Reggie Bannister? The name was familiar. *Bannister?* Then he remembered. Child custody case where the mother had shacked up with a known drug dealer and become addicted to meth. Bannister was the father and wanted his kids out of there. Dallas helped the man gain sole custody of his sons by conducting surveillance on the mother. A month later she was found in a rundown motel on the outskirts of town. She'd been dead for a couple of weeks and the local rats had feasted.

"Yeah, I remember Mr. Bannister," Dallas said. "How's he doing?"

"Very well," Melanie Treadwell replied. "He told me that his sons are doing well and to give you his regards."

"That's nice. I liked him. Glad his boys are safe with him."

"Yes."

After a short, static pause he broke the silence. "Ms. Treadwell, I'm sure you didn't call just to pass on Reggie's well wishes."

"Yes, you're right about that, Mr. Harper."

He used a line that he'd pulled from some Tom Cruise movie when people called him that: "Every time you say Mr. Harper I look around for my dad. I'm Dallas."

"All right, then, Dallas," she continued. "Look, I just don't know where to turn. I need help and Reggie said you might be a good resource."

"I appreciate his confidence," Dallas said. "I guess it depends on what you need help with."

Another uncomfortable pause, longer this time. Then, "Can we meet in person to discuss this? I think I'd be more comfortable with that."

Dallas glanced at his watch. Almost eight. "Sure. Where and when?"

"The Waterside Café at nine," she said without hesitation. "Do you know where that is?"

"No."

He uncapped a nearby pen with his teeth and scribbled the address on his palm.

"Got it," he mumbled with the pen cap still stuck between his teeth.

"Thank you, Mr. Harper."

"Dallas," he tried reminding her, but she was gone.

• • •

Most of what she'd told him had been the truth.

Reggie Bannister had indeed said that Dallas Harper helped him gain full custody of his sons. It was also true that she hadn't contacted Harper simply to say hi from Bannister. There was more to it than that. Much more.

The only real lie she told Harper was her name. She'd literally made Melanie Treadwell up in the nervous seconds before he answered the phone. The woman probably existed somewhere, it just wasn't her.

She didn't want to give him her real name. Not yet at least. As a private investigator she figured he'd be able to trace her true identity in no time. With "Melanie Treadwell," if he checked, all he'd run into is an anonymous dead end. This way she maintained the upper hand. If she wanted to tell him the truth behind her sudden appearance in his life she could. If not, she would simply vanish like a ghost.

Part of her didn't know why she was in Florida doing this. What good would it do? Then again, what real harm could come of this? Besides, she wanted to know the truth, and what better place to start than with Dallas Harper Investigations. One way or another he was the man who could provide her with the closure she needed.

19

The Truth about Melanie

Dallas found the Waterside Café on the Channel Riverwalk, a palm-dotted harbor with cobblestone walkways and marbled alcoves overlooking Tampa Bay. Whoever the mysterious Melanie Treadwell was she picked a nice place for breakfast.

After hanging up with her he did a quick records search. No Melanie Treadwell listed in Tampa. In fact, no one by that name in all of Florida. He expanded it to a nationwide search and came up with two dozen women by that name, the closest of whom lived in Tennessee. He wasn't surprised. In his line of work aliases were common. He'd eventually get her real name, but for now he'd play along to see what she wanted.

It was probably some sort of cheating husband deal, he thought. Easy enough. He could work that kind of case in his sleep. He'd follow the guy for a couple weeks, record all his illicit liaisons, and then present the damning info to Melanie Treadwell, or whatever her real name was. He didn't care what she called herself as long as her check was good.

Before leaving the house he showered quickly and slipped into his work attire: khaki Dockers, red polo shirt, and sport coat. Beneath the coat he packed a 9mm Beretta strapped to a beat-up leather holster with two extra magazines on the right side. On the left hung a pair of Peerless handcuffs.

He'd learned one very important thing early on in his career: a gun wasn't any good without a set of cuffs. You could hold people at gunpoint for only so long before a) you had to shoot them, or b) they simply ran away, knowing you had no real reason to shoot them and you had no other way to subdue them.

Since most of his case work involved surveillance and intelligence gathering the gun and cuffs rarely came out. Still, as a private investigator, you never knew when something bad was going to happen. One thing he learned in the police academy before getting kicked out was action always beats reaction. A bad guy knew what he was going to do before you, the good guy, did. As a result, your reaction to him was always a fraction of a second behind his initial action. Now that he thought about it, there were two other things he remembered. The reactionary gap for an attacker with a knife was twenty-one feet. Why that stuck in his head he had no idea. Perhaps the most important thing he learned during his short tenure with the LAPD was quite simple: never sleep with the chief of police's daughter.

• • •

She watched him stroll through the front door, his eyes darting warily from side to side. He looked different in person; taller, older, more handsome in a rugged kind of way. She supposed the touch of gray around his temples in an otherwise full head of dark hair gave him that distinguished look. Before today the only image she'd seen of him had been lifted from his Web site. Now that he was here in person she had a hard time believing it was really him.

Their eyes met and he nodded and smiled warmly.

"Ms. Treadwell?"

She extended her hand and stood. "Yes. And you're obviously Mr. Harper."

"Dallas," he gently reminded her.

She smiled. "Yes, Dallas. I'm sorry."

"No problem."

He took a seat at the table and surveyed the restaurant. Moderately busy with half a dozen other patrons seated nearby. A man and woman, both casually dressed, with a newborn slumbering in a car seat on the floor next to them. Behind them, two men dressed in dark suits poring over a pile of paperwork spread out across the table. Ten feet to his right sat an older man, alone, reading the newspaper and sipping on a ceramic mug of steaming coffee. Dallas looked closer and noticed the man's white collar. He supposed priests liked to go out for breakfast too.

The restaurant itself was well lit and decorated with dark woods and bright colors. Almost a tropical craftsman look. Trendy yet classic. Kind of like Melanie Treadwell. Early twenties, fit, with shoulder-length dark hair that framed her high cheekbones. There was something vaguely familiar about her, but he quickly dismissed the thought. He was sure he'd never seen her before. Still, something nagged at the back of his mind, soft like a whisper.

"Thanks for meeting me here," Melanie said. "I know it's short notice but I really thought it would be better if we spoke in person."

Dallas folded his hands, steepling his index fingers beneath his chin. "Well, I'd be lying if I said I wasn't intrigued by your phone call this morning."

She pursed her lips and nodded. "I suppose I did come off sounding a bit mysterious."

"Yeah, a bit," he replied.

Before she could answer Kyle, the waiter, interrupted. Dallas ordered scrambled eggs, biscuits and gravy, and a cup of coffee. Melanie asked for a cappuccino and an English muffin, lightly buttered. After Kyle left, Melanie spoke.

"Where to start," she murmured.

Dallas leaned in and crossed his forearms on the table. "How about with your real name?" he said, sternly, but not unfriendly.

The look on her face showed she was taken aback. She leaned back and crossed her arms. "Not yet," she said. "Eventually I will, but not until I'm one hundred percent certain you're the man I'm looking for."

The way she phrased that last part puzzled him. She was looking for him? Maybe there was no cheating hubby running all over town.

"I guess I'm not following you," Dallas said, eyeing her suspiciously.

She sighed and leaned forward. "I'm sorry. I'm not good at this kind of stuff."

"Look, Ms. Treadwell, you contacted me, OK. I mean, I'm not trying to sound like a prick or anything, but there had to be a reason for you calling me. And don't give me this song and dance about Reggie Bannister sending his best. You probably read his testimonial on my Web site. I'm sure that's how you got his name."

A pensive nod floated across the table as she nervously chewed her bottom lip. Then, the truth came out in a torrent. "I'm from Los Angeles, Mr. Harper, and my real name is Allison Braxton. It's taken me a long time to track you down. You knew my mother a long time ago. Roxanne Braxton. I think you're my biological father...."

20

Father Bill

Father Bill Kinney couldn't help but overhear what was going on at the table ten feet away from his. He hoped his eavesdropping wasn't obvious. His ears had perked up when the man said he wasn't trying to be a prick about something. He tuned in to the rest of the conversation purely by accident and was taken aback by the young woman's revelation a few moments later. What a way to find out you had a long-lost daughter. Over breakfast at the Waterside Café.

He hoped that didn't happen to him someday. He'd been less than chaste before deciding on a career in the ministry at the age of thirty. A disturbing scenario began playing out in his mind.

He's in the confessional absolving his flock of their sins when a young woman walks in. Since she's seated behind a screen he can't see her face. Her voice is soft, young, and she stammers with uncertainty. Then, the bombshell: in college he knew her mother. *Knew* her mother. It had taken her years to find him but here she was, his daughter. Father Bill Kinney had a daughter. The scandal would send shock waves rippling through his congregation. There would be righteous outrage and calls for an investigation. Maybe even demands that he turn in his collar, just like in the movies when a cop is told to turn in his badge and gun to the captain.

"Refill, Father?"

The waiter's voice broke the reverie.

"Oh, yes, please. Thanks."

After the waiter left, Father Kinney disengaged himself from the paternity conversation at the table to his left and went back to skimming through the daily news. Roadside bombs in Iraq, eighty people killed. Car bombs in Afghanistan. Tension in Israel between Jews and Palestinians. Drug wars south of the border in Mexico. Kim Jong Il acting like a petulant child in North Korea. Hugo Chavez doing the same only in South America.

Same shit, different day, he thought.

Sometimes he wondered what God was thinking. It seemed like this whole humanity experiment had gone terribly wrong. People killing each other over territory, oil, drugs, hurt feelings. Albert Einstein had once said that insanity was doing the same thing over and over again and expecting different results. By that definition, humanity suffered from the most severe, irreparable form of psychosis. Still, the world kept on spinning.

He folded the front page and smoothed it shut on the table top. Sports was next. Rays lost. Buccaneers won. Brett Favre was making another comeback, this time in the Canadian Football League. He was about to start reading a story about academic fraud at Florida State University when the thought hit him. It wasn't a bad idea. The more he mulled it over the more he liked it. Characters were beginning to swirl in his mind. The intrepid daughter; the long-lost father who had become a priest; fate bringing them together. All with a spiritual undercurrent. It could make a great novel. Just the kind of project he'd been looking for.

Over the years he'd published three books on the history of Christianity. He'd always wanted to delve into the fiction side of the business but the inspiration hadn't been there. Until now.

He reached into his breast pocket, pulled out a notebook and pen and began scribbling notes. After five minutes he had a rough outline; ten minutes after that the main characters had materialized. By the time he phoned his agent from his office at the rectory he already had the first chapter written.

New York

21

Divine Inspiration

"I tell you, Bill, that's a hell of an idea," Marty Goldstein said in a voice made rough and gravelly from too many cigarettes and three-martini lunches. He scrolled through the first few pages of the priest's e-mail. "I think you've got a winner on your hands."

"Thanks, Marty," Father Bill Kinney said from the other end of the line eleven hundred miles away in Tampa. "It's the kind of breakthrough I've been looking for. And it all hit me while I was eating breakfast."

"Tell me about it."

Father Bill told him all about the Waterside Café and the young woman who had just found her father.

"Divine inspiration, my friend," Goldstein said as he laughed. He shifted in his chair, adjusting his sizable girth. *Really should lose some weight*, he thought. "That's how it happens with all the great ones. Hemingway. Steinbeck. Hell, even the Beatles. Didn't Paul McCartney write one of their biggest hits on the back of a napkin?"

"Yeah," Kinney replied. "I think it was 'Hey Jude.' I guess you never know where or when inspiration will strike. Kind of like Saul on the road to Damascus."

"Was that the guy who's wife got turned into a pillar of salt?"

"*Oy vey*," Father Bill muttered, laughing. "No, Marty, that was Lot. Saul was the guy who changed his name to Paul. He wrote half the stuff in the New Testament."

"Oh, OK," Goldstein muttered sheepishly. "Guess I should have read your other books a bit more carefully."

"Did you read them at all?"

A pause from the other end of the line, followed by a jocular, "So, how about those Buccaneers."

Father Bill laughed. "That's OK, Marty. I'm sure whoever read those manuscripts learned a great deal about the early Church."

"Yeah, Elaine Harris probably did."

They chatted for a few more minutes before saying their good-byes. Marty had always enjoyed talking with Bill Kinney. He considered the priest a good friend. Plus the man's books had sold well, helping put The Goldstein Agency on the literary map ten years earlier.

With the phone back in its cradle he swiveled his chair around and gazed out from his forty-story perch. An ocean of buildings stretched as far as the eye could see. Some probably thought it was an eyesore; a testimonial to what was wrong with the world. He saw things completely different. To him, the sprawling panorama of midtown Manhattan with its skyscrapers, offices, apartment buildings, and corner stores was a testament to humanity's ingenuity. It was no less beautiful than the Grand Canyon or Yellowstone National Park. Just breathtaking in its own gritty way.

A random memory of his father floated through his consciousness. Instinctively, he glanced to his left. Plastered to the wall was a tattered Nazi flag, its large, black swastika snarling in the muted light of Goldstein's office. Other than his wife and kids, the flag was perhaps his most prized possession. His father had pulled it off the family room wall of the commandant's house at Dachau. Bernard Goldstein was one of the first American liberators to breach the walls of the death camp. He had fought his way across Europe, wallowing in blood and body parts along the way, but nothing could have prepared him for what he saw at Dachau. That was beyond horror—beyond all human comprehension. He'd snatched the flag as a solemn reminder to never forget what atrocities had occurred behind those razor-wire walls.

Marty turned away from the Manhattan skyline and reached for his cell phone. He punched in a number he'd memorized long ago and waited. Three rings and she answered.

"What are you wearing?" Marty asked.

The woman on the other end of the line giggled playfully. "Wouldn't you like to know?"

"As a matter of fact, I would. You busy?"

"Not too busy for you."

He felt himself stiffening so he shifted things around. She had that effect on him. "How about a little afternoon delight?" he said.

"Aren't you a naughty boy?" came her reply. "What would your wife say?"

"I won't tell if you don't."

"My lips are sealed," she said, breathlessly. "The Marriott downtown? One hour?"

"See you then."

Another playful laugh and the connection died.

•   •   •

They made love urgently in room 235, their usual rendezvous location. Sloppy, wet kisses dissolved into slower more passionate ones. He entered her an instant later, thrusting deep inside her, faster and faster, until they both came in a blinding rush. They repeated the sequence three more times during the next hour.

Sated, spent, Marty rolled onto his back and pulled the bed sheets over his legs. The woman turned on her side and began running her fingers through his coarse mat of chest hair. His body still tingled from the intense lovemaking. In his head he could hear the rhythmic palpitation of his racing heart as it pulled blood away from his loins and redistributed it more evenly throughout his body.

"Was it good for you, baby?" she purred.

"Incredible," he muttered breathlessly. "You're amazing."

Her laugh was melodic. "You weren't too bad, yourself. Did you learn some new moves since last time?"

He glanced to his left taking in the delicate contours of her face. At that moment she was the most beautiful woman he'd ever seen.

"Maybe," he smirked. "Actually, I picked up this book and read about a couple of new techniques. Guess it paid off."

"Definitely." She smiled as she rolled onto her back and stretched.

Marty turned to the nightstand next to the bed and grabbed his wallet. From inside the folds he pulled five crisp one hundred dollar bills and pressed them into her palm.

"Thanks," she replied as she took the money and slipped into her clothes. "See you at home tonight."

"You bet, honey," Marty said to his wife of twenty years. "Want me to pick anything up on the way home?"

"A loaf of bread, a carton of milk, and a stick of butter."

They both laughed at the inside joke.

"No," Ruth Goldstein finally said. "Just get your cute butt home before seven. The Jensens are stopping over."

"No problem."

• • •

Outside, the sidewalks were choked with knots of migrating humanity; the streets were like clogged arteries. In front of the hotel, amid the bustle and noise, Marty Goldstein stood hailing a cab. Two cabbies zipped past him, weaving dangerously in and out of traffic like NASCAR drivers. Finally, the third taxi he waved down pulled to the curb and he got in.

"To where?" the cabbie asked, his Middle-Eastern accent as thick as hummus. The guy even smelled like the pasty mélange of chick peas, garlic, and tahini, Marty thought as he glanced at the man's taxi license on the front dash: Mohammed Mohammed Kus Imak.

Marty told him and reclined in the threadbare leather seat with the memories of the early afternoon sex romp still burning fresh in his mind. It was a little game he and Ruth started playing two years earlier to spice up their marriage. And it had worked. They had never been closer, more in sync with each other. He attributed part of that to the safely illicit trysts where he played the John and she was his high-end call girl. Sometimes they mixed it up a bit. Different hotels, his office, public bathrooms. Nothing was out of bounds. And why should it be.

"Day is nice, yes," Mohammed Mohammed said from the front seat.

Marty nodded absently. "Yeah, it is. Supposed to rain tomorrow though."

The cabbie nodded uncertainly, and then smiled.

For the next two blocks they rode in silence, Marty still basking in the delicious afterglow of naughty lovemaking while the cabbie's eyes nervously connected the dots between his side mirror, the rearview mirror, and the passenger side mirror.

At least he's not driving like a maniac, Marty thought. *Pretty cautious for a New York taxi driver. Especially one who's probably more used to riding a camel than driving a car.*

Stop it. He felt bad for thinking that. To appease his nagging conscience he dropped the detached act.

"Where are you from?" he asked the cabbie.

Mohammed Mohammed glanced in the rearview mirror. "Israel," he said. "West Bank town of Nablus. I am Palestinian."

"I see."

Great, another towelhead. Probably has a bomb strapped to his chest as we speak.

Stop it! His conscience was more insistent this time.

Mohammed Mohammed eased the cab to a stop at a red light. "You from New York?" he asked. "Your nose look Jewish."

Marty laughed out loud. Stereotypes went both ways.

"Yes, I'm Jewish," he answered. "Although my nose doesn't look any bigger than yours, my friend."

This time Mohammed Mohammed laughed. "We are cousins. Arabs and Jews from Abraham."

Marty nodded. He knew at least that much about his heritage: Arabs and Jews were both Semitic.

"When did you come to America?" Marty asked.

The light turned green and the cabbie accelerated through the intersection.

"One month," he said, holding up his index finger. "My wife and children still in Nablus."

"Why didn't they come with you?"

"Someday, *Inshallah*," Mohammed Mohammed replied. "First, I need work and get apartment. Then, I get visa for them."

"That must be hard," Marty said. He could see the puzzled look on the cabbie's face in the rearview mirror.

"Hard? What means this?"

Marty sat up. "Difficult. It must be very difficult to be so far away from your family."

Recognition dawned in Mohammed Mohammed's eyes. "Ah, yes, difficult. Very difficult. I miss my family. But, I do all this for them. Come to America for better life. In Nablus, nothing. No work. People lazy. Always blame Israel and Jews for the problems. Not everything Israel's fault. Some things, yes, but not everything. I want better thing for my family."

Marty felt even worse now for his less than kind thoughts about the Arab cab driver. Mohammed Mohammed seemed like a decent guy. Hard working, ambitious. He had guts too. Coming to a foreign country in search of a new life couldn't be easy. Especially when you had to leave everything you knew and loved behind.

"Well, good luck," Marty said as the cab came to a halt in front of his building. He flipped the cabbie a fifty and told him to keep the change. "I hope it all works out for you."

"Thank you, my friend." The cabbie smiled warmly. "You are very generous. May *Allah* smile upon you."

22

The Last Fare

Mohammed Mohammed was supposed to be done working at midnight. Twelve hours of dodging rude, middle-finger-wagging drivers and oblivious pedestrians was enough. All he wanted to do was go back to his rundown studio apartment in Harlem and throw his weary body on the dirty mattress he'd gotten last week. It was nice to finally have something to sleep on. Before finding the mattress in the alley behind his building he'd slept on layers of old rags he managed to scrounge from around the cab stand. Americans were so wasteful. They threw perfectly good things away, like the mattress, and food. He'd never seen so much food in his life. So much discarded food too. What people in Nablus said about America was true: it was indeed the land of plenty.

Two miles from the cab stand Mohammed Mohammed saw a young black man dressed in saggy dark pants, an oversized white T-shirt and a New York Yankees baseball cap canted to the left. As the gap narrowed between the two the black man raised his right hand. Mohammed Mohammed was tempted to keep driving and skip this fare. He was tired. Then, he thought of his family. Every fare he snagged brought him one step closer to bringing them to New York. To America, the land of plenty. The fare might not be much—a few dollars, maybe—but it was that much more money in his pocket. Every little bit counted.

He changed lanes and eased the cab to the curb. The black man smiled and hopped in the back seat.

"Hello, my friend," Mohammed Mohammed said with a smile. He pushed the fatigue out of his voice. He'd figured out during his short time as a New York cabbie that smiles and pleasant chatter brought in bigger tips.

"Yo, what's up?" the young black man mumbled.

Mohammed Mohammed had heard that greeting before but still had no idea what it meant. *What's up?* Many things. The sky. Trees. The moon. He'd have to ask someone about the meaning of that phrase.

"To where?" the cabbie asked. He glanced in the rearview mirror. Something icy skittered down his spine.

The man in the back pulled out a small handgun and pressed the cold barrel to Mohammed Mohammed's temple. "Pull around the corner, motherfucker," he growled.

Mohammed Mohammed didn't panic. He'd had guns pointed at him before. Much bigger guns, held by Jews and Arabs alike. He knew enough to not be a hero, though. The *Abid* probably just wanted money. As hard as it would be to part with his earnings for the day, it would be much harder for him to part with his life.

Then what would his wife and children do? They would be stuck in Nablus forever. He wasn't going to let that happen.

"You want money, I have money," Mohammed Mohammed told the young man behind him as he pulled the cab around the corner.

"You goddamn right I want yo money," the thug replied. "Why the fuck else you think I be here?"

Mohammed Mohammed had a hard enough time understanding and communicating in regular English. His English-Ebonics comprehension was much worse.

"I will give it to you..." he started reaching into his pocket but the thug stopped him short.

"Don't go sticking your hand in that pocket," he snarled. "You probably got a gun in there. Or a bomb, you Al-Qaeda motherfucker."

This Abid is obsessed about intercourse with his mother, Mohammed Mohammed thought. Typical. No wonder sub-Sahara Africa was such a mess. They acted like animals.

"No gun. No bomb. I will give you money and then you leave me."

The black thug laughed. "Shit, I'll take your money and whatever else I want. What you gonna do about it?" The last part sounded more like *Watchugonnadoboudit.*

The Palestinian raised his hands. "Please, take the money and go. I have a family."

The thug grinned, his teeth gleaming in the muted glow of the overhead street light like razor wire. "Man, shit, I don't give a fuck about you and your family. Fuck you. Fuck all of you towelhead motherfuckers."

Mohammed Mohammed was about to say something but he stopped. The look in the thug's eyes changed. Whatever reason had been there was gone. The only thing that shone behind the thug's eyes now was contempt, undiluted and psychotic.

"No, please," Mohammed Mohammed mumbled under his breath.

"Shut the fuck up."

In the darkness the Arab began to pray. He had just asked *Allah* for forgiveness of all his sins when the first bullet slammed into the back of his head. He was dead by the time the second round sprayed the rest of his brains across the dashboard and windshield.

23

Blood in, Blood out

The killer's real name was DeLonzo Peeples but all his homies called him Peep. He was a proud member of The Tre-Deuce Boyz, one of Harlem's most ruthless street gangs. At least *now* he was a member. Killing the towelhead made his membership a certainty. The council had given him the choice: get jumped into the TDBs or put in work for the gang. He chose the latter. The cabbie just happened to be in the wrong place at the wrong time. If it hadn't been the sand nigger, it would have been some other nigger. That's just how he rolled. He didn't give a fuck.

After popping a cap in the cabbie's head he fled the area on foot, dipping in and out of alleys and yards like a shadow in the dark. He knew the area better than the back of his hand. This was his 'hood; twenty square blocks of crack houses, whores, junkies, hustlers, and bangers. And now, he'd be helping run the drug trade in TDC territory, as well as other gang business. Guns, prostitution, protection. Not too bad for a fifteen-year-old.

Somewhere near 126th Street he ducked into a dark alley. In the distance gunshots rang out, six of them, followed by a shotgun blast, incoherent shouting, and the squeal of tires. The sirens came a few seconds after that.

As he sauntered down the alley he smiled. He loved the chaos of the 'hood. It was all he knew. Family for him wasn't like it was for most people. Mom, Dad, brothers, sisters. For him family was his set: T-Bone, Renzo, Toe, Mookie, Dre, Broom and all the other Boyz. Life was a merry-go-round of drugs, money, ho's and violence.

Midway down the alley he ducked through a dilapidated wooden fence. A pit bull nearby went crazy, barking and frothing at the mouth as it tugged against the thick chain that kept it tethered to a steel spike anchored solidly to the ground.

"Shut the fuck up, Dawg," Peep muttered.

The dog, recognizing its master's voice, quieted and dropped submissively to the ground. Peep ran a hand under the canine's chin and scratched. Dawg's front right paw began thumping involuntarily.

"Who's there?" The deep voice came right after the rear porch light illuminated the backyard.

Peep shielded his eyes against the harsh glare. "Damn, dawg, shut that off. It's just me."

"Peep?"

"Yup. All is well, G."

The light went out and Peep went inside. Seated around the kitchen table were Renzo, Toe, Mookie, and Broom playing cards. Dre stood by the twisted screen door. "You get it done?" he asked.

Peep nodded proudly. "It's all good. Wet some motherfucking towelhead cab driver. Got this too." He held up a wad of bills, mainly twenties with one fifty in the mix.

"No Benjamins, homey?" Renzo asked from the card game.

"Shit," Peep mumbled. "You want some Benjamins you go get 'em."

Renzo leaned back in wooden chair and laughed. "Fuck that," he said, pulling a roll of one hundred dollar bills from his pocket. "I got mine, bitch."

This time all the gangsters laughed. Dre pulled Peep to the table and pushed a chair his way. "Let's deal the old boy in," he said. "Maybe take away some of that pretty green he's flashing."

Toe shuffled the deck and flipped five cards to each man around the table. After the discard Renzo won the five hundred dollar pot with three jacks. While the rest of the TDBs bantered with each other, Dre leaned in and whispered in Peep's ear. "Ain't no turning back now, G. Blood in, blood out."

Peep glanced sideways at his criminal mentor and nodded slowly. "Blood in, blood out," he repeated. "Blood in, blood out."

24

Numb

Sergeant Danny Heath should have been home six hours ago. Instead, he was at his second homicide of the day, this one a cab driver shot point-blank in the back of the head. So far, the report was going to read like so many other murders in New York: Victim DOA, no suspect info. That's how it was with a lot of these random killings. The administration liked to tell people that every case was important and would be worked until there were no more leads. The reality was quiet different. Unless you were caught standing over the body with the murder weapon in hand, chances are you were going to get away scot-free. That wasn't a knock on NYPD detectives. They were some of the best investigators in the world. It was simply a matter of too many killers and not enough cops.

"Do we have a positive ID on this guy?" Heath asked his partner, Joey Toscano.

"Yeah," Toscano muttered absently as he flipped through a small notebook. "Uh.——Mohammed Mohammed Kus Imak. Poor bastard.

Been here for a month. Came from somewhere in Israel. Boss said he was a good guy. Hard worker."

Danny shook his head sadly but felt nothing inside. This job had changed him in so many ways over the years. Human suffering and misery no longer affected him. The lyrics to the Pink Floyd tune "Comfortably Numb" sing-songed through his head. He'd loved that song as a morose teenager. In fact, the whole album was great. *The Wall*. He used to sit, headphones plastered to his ears, and listen to it for hours. Those days had been much simpler. A time before he knew about rapists, killers, and gangbangers.

Before he knew that a dead body would bloat and seep rancid juice and gasses if it stewed undiscovered too long in the simmering heat of summer. Before he knew that there were men out there who would sodomize children and slit their tiny throats when it was all over.

"What about next of kin?" Heath asked.

"Nada," Toscano replied. "Apparently, this guy was working to bring his wife and kids here. At least that's what his boss said. This guy had no one here. All his relatives are back home."

Danny slipped his hands into a pair of rubber gloves and opened the driver's door of the cab. The scent of violent death greeted him, warm and coppery. Crime Lab would be here any minute to process the scene. After that the medical examiner would tag and bag the stiff and have the car towed to the Forensics Garage. All in all, it was a pretty routine case. As routine as homicide could be, he supposed.

Danny removed the gloves and tossed them in the gutter. "What are we up to now?"

Toscano's brow furrowed. "What do you mean?"

"This homicide, how many does that give us?"

"Oh. Shit, it's got to be 867. Our last one was 865, and then there was that one an hour after that. The gay domestic."

"I think you're right. We should top one thousand murders easily this year. Maybe even fifteen hundred the way things have been going lately."

It had been a brutal summer on the streets of New York. After reaching all-time lows in homicide in the late 1990s, the city had seen a resurgence in gang violence over the last few years. Steady increases in violent crime each year during the early part of the twenty-first century had finally brought New York's homicide rate back to where it was in the mid-1980s. Back then two thousand killings a year was the norm. It looked like the crime economy had recovered; it was a bull market for murder.

"Do you want to look at anything else here?" Toscano asked.

As the senior investigator, Heath was the incident commander.

"No, I think we're good," Danny replied. "Can you and Morales handle this one? I'm beat. I haven't had a day off in two weeks."

Morales was Sergeant Christina Morales. She and Toscano had been an item last year until his wife found out about their relationship. Mrs. Toscano put an end to everything by walking out on her husband and taking the kids, house, most of his 403b account and half of his pension. Morales didn't stick around either. She jumped ship, shacking up with a street cop from the Eighty-fifth Precinct a month after Joey Toscano's divorce was finalized. He still got to see the kids one weekend a month. The way his ex had poisoned their minds, that was fine with him.

The junior sergeant nodded and smiled. "No problem. I could use the overtime. Plus, maybe Tina wants to pick up where we left off."

Danny shook his head slowly. "Joey, don't."

"I'm kidding, Danny." Toscano smiled. "I've sworn off women forever."

It was Danny's turn to laugh. "Yeah, right. Since when?"

"Yesterday. After that waitress I've been seeing suddenly went nuts talking about marriage."

"Which waitress?" Danny asked. "The one from The Uptowner or the one from Al's?"

Toscano thought for a moment before answering. "Al's. I think."

"I give you a week," Danny said, a narrow smirk drawn across his lips.

"A week?" Toscano laughed louder this time. "Shows how well you know me. That's longer than I'm giving myself, bro."

• • •

The squad room was deserted, except for Mike Mallory in the far corner who sat composing a report on his computer one finger at a time. He nodded absently at Danny as he entered the room and immediately went back to typing.

Danny tossed his briefcase on top of his desk and sank into his chair. It felt good to finally sit down; his lower back was killing him. Maybe a much-needed massage tomorrow. He wasn't coming in to work no matter what happened. Not even if the whole damn city was burning down. And the way things had been going lately, that was a distinct possibility.

"You should go home," Mallory said from across the room. "You look like shit."

"I wish I felt that good," Danny chuffed. He undid his tie and kicked his feet up.

"What about you? You've been here longer than me today."

Mallory swung around in his chair and leaned back, fingers entwined behind his head. "I've got to get this report done for that assault in the park. I want to get those assholes charged ASAP."

From the opposite corner a portable squawked to life as the disembodied voice of a dispatcher sent a squad to an armed robbery in progress.

"You ever miss those days?" Mallory asked, tipping his head toward the radio. "Running from call to call. No breaks. Jumping out on shitheads on the corner."

Danny shrugged. "Sometimes, I guess. At least there you don't have to take your work home with you. You handle the call, clear and then go on to the next one. Not like working these cases." He thumped a stack of papers on his desk. "I don't think this pile has ever been less than a foot thick."

Mallory nodded, grinned. "Tell me about it. But look on the bright side: as long as there's junkies, killers, robbers, hookers, and gangsters we've got job security."

"That's one way to look at it."

Danny planted his feet beneath his desk and signed on to his computer. A few moments later he was into his work e-mail account. Fifteen new ones, nine of which were obviously junk mail. He deleted those without reading them. The next two were memos from the chief reaffirming his support of the troops in light of the latest scandal to rock the department. Blah, blah, blah. Typical politician, Danny thought. Playing both sides. He deleted both of those.

The next one was from his brother, a joke. He read it and laughed. He moved the cursor across the computer screen and clicked Forward. Norm Turner, his former partner and the newly appointed chief of police in Surprise, Arizona, would appreciate this. He had a warped sense of humor too.

Surprise

25

Mental Health Outsourcing

Norm Turner placed the Grande Starbucks vanilla latte on top of his neatly manicured desk and took a seat. Everything was in its place, just as he'd left it last night before leaving work. Family photo on the right corner of the desk, a framed picture of him in his newly pressed chief's uniform, shaking hands with the mayor, balancing things on the left side. In the middle, facing out, sat a brass name-plate his wife had made for him: Norman A. Turner, Chief of Police. Laptop in the middle, phone next to that and that was it. Pens and highlighters sat organized by color in one of the desk drawers, next to a stapler and scissors. That was about all he needed in the way of office gear. His secretary, Kari Turner—no relation—kept all the big guns housed in her desk outside his office door in the foyer.

Turner didn't like clutter. His parents had been notorious pack rats, hoarding magazines, newspapers, empty cardboard boxes, old clothes and shoes, and electronic equipment from Thomas Edison's laboratory. Long ago he'd run in the opposite direction shunning all knickknacks and tossing anything that had worn out its usefulness.

After reading a newspaper or magazine he threw it in the recycle bin. Any item of clothing he'd gone a year without wearing got donated to the Salvation Army. Empty boxes were flattened and tossed in the compactor out back in the squad bay. Fastidious didn't accurately describe Chief Turner. Psychotically organized was a better description.

Although some poked fun at him, Turner's organizational skills had served him well during his career in law enforcement, first working the gritty streets of New York as a patrol officer, and then as a homicide detective. If his office was a model of institutional efficiency, his mind was even more so. Even in there everything had its place.

It was still early, seven fifteen, and the rest of the building was quiet. Norm liked this time of day, before the bustle began. He'd always been a morning person, preferring to watch the sun rise after a good night's sleep as opposed to watching it rise after being up all night chasing bad guys.

Outside, past the air-conditioned comfort of his modest office, the desert baked. Ninety already and it wasn't even midmorning. Summer in the Valley of the Sun was nothing like summer back in New York. Here, it was a broiler. Still, this place was paradise compared to the concrete jungle a continent away. A jungle he'd been more than happy to leave last year after bagging the top cop job in Surprise, thirty minutes northwest of downtown Phoenix. Everything here was better. Cleaner air, nicer people, and more affordable housing. Their three-bedroom house behind the ninth tee box in Coyote Lakes cost three times less than their one-bedroom condo in New York. And golf here wasn't something you could do only a few months of the year. Here, in the shadow of the White Tank Mountains, you could hit the links year round. Heaven, as far as Chief Turner was concerned.

He logged on to his computer and accessed his e-mails. The one from his old partner caught his attention immediately.

From: Heath, Daniel
To: Turner, Norman
Subject: Mental Health Outsourcing

I was depressed last night so I called Lifeline. Got a call center in Pakistan. Told them I was suicidal. They got all excited and asked if I could drive a truck.

Turner leaned back in his chair and laughed. Good one. Typical Danny: political correctness be damned.

He reached for his cell phone and thumbed in Danny's number. Three weeks since they'd last talked. Way too long. He'd tried his best to convince Danny to pull up stakes and head out west to God's country. Danny said he'd think about it. Maybe he'd be able to talk him into it this time, Turner thought.

Danny picked up after three rings. "Hello."

"Don't tell me you're still sleeping," Turner chided his old partner. "It's seven thirty here. That' means it's nine thirty there."

"You woke me up, you bastard," Danny said in a tone heavy with sleep.

"What? You're not at work yet catching killers?"

From the other end of the line movement and a husky cough. "I took the day off," Danny explained. "Worked twenty straight hours the past couple of days on two homicides. I planned on sleeping all day. Until you called and woke me up."

"You're a glutton for punishment," Turner said. "I told you last time you should retire and head out here and work for me. I'm still looking for a lieutenant in investigations."

"Yeah?"

Turner could tell by the tone of Heath's voice that the detective was interested. And why not? It was a great job. Sure, he'd take a small pay cut, but that would be more than offset by his NYPD pension.

"Yup. And the only person you'd have to answer to would be me."

A chuckle from the other end. "Is that supposed to sell me on the idea? You were kind of a jerk as a partner. Not sure how I'd feel with you as my boss."

Turner laughed loudly. "Man, you're stubborn. Look, how many homicides are you guys sitting on right now?"

Danny told him.

"You know what," Turner continued," we haven't had that many in the whole history of Surprise. We've had one this year. You've probably investigated more by yourself in the last week."

"Can't argue with that," Danny replied.

"Then quit punishing yourself and get out here. Put your two weeks in and submit your pension paperwork. You've got no one holding you there, do you?"

"Nope."

It was true. His last relationship ended badly ten months earlier after the woman (what was her name again? Tiffany) couldn't take dating a cop anymore. The hours, the sullenness, the distance. She left him for an accountant. Last he heard they'd gotten married and moved upstate.

"So, you going to pull the pin?" Turner asked.

The short pause stretched into a longer silence. Then, "OK, I'm in."

"Really?" The surprise in Turner's voice was palpable.

"What?" Danny continued. "Did you expect me to put up more of a fight?"

"Kind of. You've been saying no for so long I just figured it was a lost cause."

"Yeah, well, I think I'm finally ready. After yesterday's blood-bath. Man...I don't know...I think I've just had enough of New York. This city's a toilet. Always has been, always will be."

"Why do you think I left?" Turner's voice was softer now. "I couldn't take it anymore either. Then, when I came here, I thought I'd died and gone to heaven. Janice too. She keeps telling me how glad she is I got this job. We're exercising together, golfing a couple of times a week. She's even got me doing..."

Turner stopped short. He'd said too much.

"What?" Danny asked. "She's got you doing what?"

Turner sighed and laughed. "OK, if I tell you don't get on me about it."

"Just tell me what it is."

A short pause. "Yoga," Turner said quietly. "She's got me doing yoga."

Danny chuckled loud enough for his old partner to hear. "Yoga? You mean like swamis and turbans and Confucius?"

"Shut up. I knew I shouldn't have told you."

The laughter on Danny's end subsided. "I'm sorry, Normy. I just can't see you doing that shit."

"Hey, it's good for you. My flexibility has improved and my stress level is way down. When you get out here I'm going to make you try it."

"My ass," Danny said.

"I'll make it an official order from the chief," Turner replied slyly.

"Well, then, if that's the case, I guess I'll have to give it a shot."

"Yes, you will." As an afterthought Turner added, "You'll really like it here, Danny. I mean it. It's going to be good for you. Change your outlook on life."

"That's good," the NYPD detective replied. "I sure as hell could use that right now."

Turner glanced at his watch and then at his calendar. He was going to stop in at the day watch roll call this morning. "Hey, I've got to go. I'll drop you an e-mail with all the info on the job."

"Copy that," Heath said. "I'll talk to you later."

"Oh, Danny, one more thing," Turner said before the connection went dead.

"Yeah?"

"Love the outsourcing joke."

26

Golf Money

After lunch at *Feelio's* the chief surveyed his fiefdom, pushing the unmarked squad west on Bell Road past Coyote Lakes Parkway. He crossed the *Aqua Fria*, an arid riverbed lined with layers of parched silt, desiccated tumbleweeds, sun-bleached tree branches, and small barrel cacti, green and spiny. Another big difference between Arizona and New York. Rivers here were nothing more than bone-dry scars crisscrossing the Sonoran landscape. At least until the monsoons came—then they became raging torrents.

At Grand Avenue he went north toward Wickenburg. The scenery was mesmerizing. Mountains as far as the eye could see rising from the desert floor; organ-pipe cacti, tall and twisted, growing in places that seemed impossible to sustain life.

He was about to exit at Wittman and head back into Surprise when he saw it on the shoulder: a beat-up old Ford van, hood propped open, with a man nosing around the engine. Inside the van, four small dark faces peered out the dirty side window. In the passenger seat, a woman sat staring straight ahead oblivious of anything except for the spider web network of cracks in the windshield.

Turner slowed and pulled in behind the van. After running the vehicle he called out his location and gave the dispatcher the relevant information: Texas plate 145MIX. As he stepped out of the car the heat slapped him across the face. He didn't care if it was a dry heat, one hundred fourteen degrees was hot no matter what.

He approached the van cautiously. Even with four children in the back you never knew. Cops had been killed on traffic stops just like this one countless times. He waved and smiled at the children as he passed. Two of them smiled back. The others simply stared at him blankly.

At the front of the van Turner poked his head around the corner. "Car trouble?"

Startled, the man stood and looked nervously at Turner's badge and then down at the chief's gun. The man was in his early to midthirties, with dark features and tired eyes. Obviously Mexican and probably illegal, Turner thought. That's how it was here down on the border.

The man smiled feebly, shrugged, and held his palms out submissively. "No speak English," he muttered haltingly, the syllables fractured.

Turner smiled and nodded. "That's OK," he said in perfect Spanish. "What happened with your van?"

The man took a step back, a look of astonishment on his face. "I don't know," he replied. "We were driving down the road when I heard this loud noise come from the engine. Then, the van stopped."

Turner nodded grimly. It sounded like a tie rod. With a van this old it could be just about anything though. And one thing he learned long ago was that he was a cop not a mechanic. Best to leave that stuff to the professionals.

He told the Mexican all this. The man hung his head and absently kicked at a sun-baked patch of ground.

"What's your name?" Turner asked.

The man looked uncertainly at the chief of police and then back at the ground. "Jose," he mumbled. "Jose Chuco."

"Jose, I'm Norm." Turner smiled warmly. "Where are you going?"

"Las Vegas," Jose replied, almost too quickly. "I have family there."

Turner wanted to ask for the man's papers and green card but couldn't bring himself to do it. Instead, he simply ran him for warrants using the man's Texas driver's license. Jose and his family were most certainly undocumented. Of that, he had no doubt. He could call the head of the local INS and probably have them deported by sundown. But what would that accomplish? Other than padding his department's stats for the month, nothing. Just because you *could* do something didn't necessarily mean you *should* do it. He wondered what he would do in Jose Chuco's situation. Stay in Mexico and starve or get killed by narco-terrorists, or cross the border into America for a better life? He knew what he would choose, illegal or not.

"Do you know anybody here?"

Jose shook his head. "We're coming from El Paso."

El Paso. It was amazing they'd made it this far in the decrepit van.

"Do you have any money?" Turner asked.

Jose reached into his pocket and pulled out a wad of crumpled bills and handed them to the chief. Thirty dollars worth of tens and ones with some lint mixed in.

Turner shook his head, smiled and held his hands up. "No, no, I don't want to take your money," he explained. "I was wondering if you had money for a tow and to get the van fixed."

Law enforcement was obviously a lot different in Mexico.

The Mexican seemed surprised, but didn't argue. He stuffed the bills back into his pocket and shook his head. "That is all the money I have."

Now what? Even if they could afford the tow to a mechanic how were they going to afford the repairs? Thirty bucks and a few pieces of pocket lint weren't going to cut it.

Then he had an idea.

• • •

Back at the police garage Norm Turner took Paul Marxhausen aside.

"What's the damage going to be?" he asked the city's head mechanic.

"If they took it to a mechanic, six hundred, minimum," Marxhausen explained.

"They've got thirty bucks," Turner muttered, more to himself than the mechanic. "How much if you were to do it as a personal favor for me?"

"A personal favor for the chief, huh? Cashing in on that could be useful someday." Marxhausen wiped his greasy hands on his overalls and grinned. "I can get the part for fifty bucks and have them on the road within the hour. It'll be more than good enough to get them to Vegas, provided nothing else goes wrong with that heap."

"I'll cover the cost of the part and throw in fifty bucks for the labor," Turner said, pumping Marxhausen's hand. "Thanks a lot, Pauly. I owe you."

"Forget about it," the mechanic said. "Just buy me a beer some-time after work."

"How about during work?" Turner joked.

"Even better."

• • •

"Your van is done," Turner said in Spanish. The Chuco fam-ily was seated in the police headquarters lobby. All four children were engrossed in an episode of *SpongeBob Squarepants* playing on the small TV behind the front desk. Turner had seen this one before with his grandkids. It was the one where the maniacal Plankton sang his version of the "Fun" song.

Jose Chuco stood, dumbfounded. No one had ever done anything like this for him. Back home in Juarez, everyone was out for themselves, even the state and federal police. Acts of kindness were based more upon what someone could gain from their altruism than actually wanting to help another person.

"My mechanic fixed the problem and gave the rest of the engine a quick inspection," Turner explained. "He said everything else looked fine. Good enough to get you to Las Vegas." He paused, reached into the cargo pocket of his uniform pants and pulled something out. "This should help too."

Still speechless, Jose stared at the crisp one hundred dollar bill. "No, senor, I cannot take that. You've done enough for me already."

Turner shook his head and pressed the bill into the Mexican's palm. "Forget about it," he said. "I insist. It's going to take more than thirty dollars to get to Las Vegas. Get your kids some happy meals from McDonald's or something."

Slowly, almost suspiciously, Jose Chuco took the money. When he looked up at Turner there were tears in his eyes.

"Thank you, senor. How can I ever repay you?"

Turner waved off the gratitude. "Don't worry about it. Just get your family to Las Vegas safely. Maybe help someone else out if you ever get the chance."

Jose nodded and dabbed at his eyes with his sleeve. He would do that for sure. Someday, somehow he would help someone else in need. Maybe not right away. First, they had to get to Las Vegas and get out of the current mess they were in. A mess that no one, not even the kind police officer here, could help them out of. But once they got to Las Vegas and took care of business everything would be OK. It had to be.

• • •

From the garage bay Chief Turner watched as the Ford van sputtered out of sight.

"That was damn nice of you," Paul Marxhausen said as he sidled up to the chief.

Turner shrugged. "Just doing the right thing."

Marxhausen laughed. "That was way beyond doing the right thing."

"Not where I come from," Turner added. "I can skip golfing for one week if the money can help those folks."

"That was your golf money?"

A nod.

"Man," Marxhausen continued, "I know how much you love golfing. You're going to be sainted for this."

Turner chuckled. With the van fully out of sight he turned and clapped the mechanic on the shoulder and then glanced at his wrist-watch. "It's quitting time, Pauly. How about that beer I owe you?"

• • •

After an hour of riding in stony silence Jose's wife finally spoke.

"That was a close call," she said quietly in Spanish from the passenger seat.

Her husband nodded. "Too close. I can't believe what just happened. I thought for sure he would search the van and find the drugs."

"Maybe God was looking out for us," Maria replied.

He grunted and dismissed the thought. A green sign with white lettering on the side of the road told him that Las Vegas was one hundred miles away. Two more hours, he thought, then they would see if God was really watching out for them. Or if there even was a God at all.

Nevada

27

Sin City

They crossed into Nevada less than two hours later, rolling over Hoover Dam and into the Pacific time zone as the sun dipped below the uneven backbone of the Spring Mountains. Had his thoughts not been elsewhere, Jose Chuco might have taken the time to marvel at the gravity-arch behemoth that kept Lake Mead from spilling over into the Colorado River. Instead of wondering how on earth men built this thing, he was contemplating what awaited them in Las Vegas. It was all he had been able to think about since leaving Juarez early yesterday, and the thoughts weren't pleasant.

He didn't want to think about it, but he knew there was a very real chance that none of them—his wife and four kids—would make it out of here alive. Still, there was hope. If he did what the drug traffickers wanted why wouldn't they let them all go? All he wanted was his twelve-year-old daughter back. They had Lupe in Las Vegas and had told him he'd get her back if he successfully brought in fifty kilos of cocaine from Juarez. What could he do? Say no? They would have killed Lupe, probably after gang-raping her, and then murdered the rest of his family while he would be forced to watch. The only thing he could do was exactly what the Mexican Mafia—*La eMe*—wanted.

Juarez, his home town, had become a bloody war zone ruled by merciless cartels whose members would stop at nothing to protect their lucrative drug trade. People were tortured and killed daily in an endless orgy of violence. Headless corpses would turn up behind schools, office buildings, and even police headquarters. The drug traffickers feared no one, not even the Mexican military. In fact, many of the cartel members and associates were woven tightly into the fabric of local law enforcement and the army. In Juarez you couldn't tell the good guys from the bad guys. All you could do is stay alert, keep your head down and not go out after dark. Even if you did all those things there was still no guarantee that you'd elude the drug traffickers or that a random bullet wouldn't tear into the back of your skull. Innocent people died all the time, caught in the crossfire of a war that they wanted no part of. A war that none of them started.

In the passenger seat next to him his wife slept. So too did his children in the back. The drive had been a long and hot one. With no air-conditioning in the van they had to leave the windows open, and that provided only modest relief from the brutal desert heat outside.

Somewhere, in the nearby hills, a coyote yowled, its plaintive cry echoing off the canyon walls. To his left, daylight's last gasp cast a scarlet halo over the sawtooth rim of the surrounding peaks. He liked it here, in America. Such a big country, and peaceful. No drug thugs terrorizing everyone. He knew the United States had its problem areas, but not like back home in Juarez. There, *everywhere* was a problem area. And the rest of Mexico wasn't much better. Maybe, when this ordeal was done, he would see about staying here. Other

Mexicans did it, why couldn't he and his family? Maybe someday he could go back to Surprise and repay the police officer who had been kind enough to help them. Maybe even become a citizen there and get a job and a house with a yard where his children could play without having to worry about headless corpses, drive-by shootings, car bombings, or being kidnapped.

28

Diablo Road

The house stood embedded in a pinion grove at the terminus of *Diablo Road*, a dusty, dead-end thoroughfare that melted into the base of an eroded tabletop mesa. There were no streetlights here. The only illumination came from the full moon overhead, a blotch of silvery-white against the pitch black maw of space.

Devil's Road. The name sent a shiver down Jose's spine. Couldn't they have at least picked a place like *Smiley Face Street* or *Happy Shiny Avenue*? He wanted to laugh but couldn't. The knot of tension that had been forming in the pit of his stomach since this whole ordeal began tightened. He choked back on the urge to vomit and took a deep breath. This is it, he thought.

Except for a dim porch light, the house was dark. They were here, though, of that he was certain, and they had been very specific with their instructions. Call the number they had given him once he arrived at the house. They would bring his daughter outside and collect their cocaine. If everything was in order he would leave here with Lupe and they would all go their separate ways. He planned on following the directions to the letter. *La eMe* was not an organization you wanted mad at you.

Using his elbow he nudged his wife. She woke with a start.

"We're here," he simply said. "The kids are still sleeping in the back. If they wake up try and keep them quiet. I'm going to call them now."

She nodded but said nothing.

He pulled the cell phone they had given him and dialed up the number. Three rings and a man answered in Spanish.

"*Hola, Senor Chuco.*"

"*Hola,*" Jose replied, trying to keep his voice steady.

"We're glad you made it," the disembodied voice on the other end of the line said. "Your daughter will be happy to see you."

"How is she?" Jose asked warily.

A snort from the other end. "She is fine. No harm has come to her. Once we get what is ours she will be free to leave with you."

"Are you in the house?"

The man laughed. "Where we are is not your concern. Just do as I say and you will be out of here with your daughter very soon."

"OK," Jose replied shakily.

"Now, I want you to step out of the van," the voice instructed. "Tell your wife to stay inside with your other children. We wouldn't want to have to shoot all of them."

Jose swallowed hard and stepped outside. The gravel beneath his feet crunched loudly. Despite the pressing heat he felt cold, clammy.

"Good," the voice said. "You're doing very well, Chuco. Not much longer. Don't do anything stupid."

"I won't," he muttered softly.

An instant later they were on him, five men carrying machine guns. They seemed to materialize out of nowhere, but he knew they'd come from behind the house. Despite the circumstances Jose was encouraged; every one of the men wore dark ski masks. More than likely, that meant they intended to let him and his family live.

"You've done well, Chuco," a man at the front of the group said in a familiar voice; it was the man Jose had been talking with. He must be the leader—the *capitan*.

Jose Chuco nodded meekly. "Can I see my daughter now?"

The man shrugged. "Why not?" He called over his shoulder. Two more masked men stepped from behind the house and made their way across the darkened front yard. Between them, Lupe.

Jose's heart sank. There she was. After a month of wondering if he'd ever see her again she finally stood before him looking no worse for the wear. Tired, yes. Nervous, most definitely. But intact.

The armed men guided her to the front of the group.

"Papa," she smiled weakly.

"Lupe." He wanted to run to her and scoop her up in his arms, but he knew that was ill-advised. No sudden movements, no stupid decisions. He knew the men who stood before him meant business. They weren't the type to ask questions first and then shoot. In fact, they weren't the type to ask questions at all. Shoot first and keep on shooting until everyone was dead. That more accurately described *La eMe's* problem-solving philosophy.

"There," the leader of the group said. "You see, Chuco, your daughter is fine. We are almost done here. Where is what we are looking for? Tell us, and you will be on your way shortly."

He told them: hidden beneath the faux-leather upholstery of the bench seat in the back of the van. A few words of instruction from the leader and the rest of the men set about tearing the seat apart. Five minutes later they had what they wanted piled up on the ground in front of their leader. He hefted one of the plastic-encased brown wrappers the size of a brick and cut a slit in the top. A small amount of the white powder fell softly to the ground like snow.

"Well done, Chuco," the *capitan* said in a voice that sounded light, like he was happy he didn't have to kill them all tonight.

Jose Chuco nodded mutely.

Another flurry of instruction in Spanish and the men packed their booty into two large duffle bags and hauled them around to the back of the house. Jose heard the slamming of doors and the gentle drone of car engines starting.

"You are free to go," the *capitan* said, nodding at Lupe.

She ran to her father and hugged him tightly.

"I missed you," she wept softly, her tears soaking his cheek.

"We missed you too," Jose replied. "Let's get out of here."

He ushered her into the van. His wife took Lupe into her arms and started crying too. It was done. Now, they could be a family again.

The *La eMe* leader turned and started walking back toward the house. Jose called out to him and he stopped.

"What, Chuco?"

"Can I speak with you for a moment?"

The *capitan* nodded and sauntered slowly back to the van. He stopped within two feet of Jose, causing the Mexican's heart to beat faster.

"Speak quickly," the leader commanded.

Jose glanced at the ground, and then back at the masked man in front of him. How was he going to do this? You didn't just ask this kind of question of the Mexican Mafia. If they let you live you were supposed to thank them meekly and get the hell out of there. He was desperate though, and before he could think, the words came tumbling out.

"I have no more money," Jose explained. He pulled the lining of his pockets out to emphasize his point. "All of it was used to get here."

The *capitan* nodded slowly. After a few moments of stony silence he laughed. "You've got guts, Chuco. First, you make it here with fifty kilos of *coca* and then you ask me for money."

In that instant the Mexican feared he'd made a tragic mistake. He should have just gone back to the van and left. Instead, he had to ask this gangster, this murderer for money. *Stupid. Stupid!*

The *capitan* shook his head and reached into his pants pocket. He took out a roll of one hundred dollar bills and tossed it to Jose.

"Ten thousand should be enough to get you home," he muttered. "Maybe even get you a new van." He laughed gruffly. "I don't think this piece of junk will get you back to Juarez."

Dumbfounded, Jose stuffed the wad in his pocket and thanked the man profusely. He almost told the *capitan* that he wasn't going back to Juarez but stopped short. The less *La eMe* knew about you the better. Instead he simply turned and got back into his van. By the time he was seated behind the wheel the *capitan* was gone.

• • •

Ten minutes later, on the highway back to Phoenix, the cell phone in his pocket rang, causing him to jump. He'd forgotten to give it back.

"Yes?"

"Chuco." It was the *capitan*.

"*Si.*"

"You have my cell phone," the gangster said.

"S-s-sorry," Jose stammered. "I forgot I had it."

"That's OK, you can keep it," the capitan said. A short pause from the other end of the line, followed by a slurry of jumbled voices in the background.

"Keep it?"

"Yes, keep it. I may have more work for you in the future."

With that the line went dead.

29

El Capitan

Miguel Morales terminated the connection and stuffed the cell phone back in his pocket. He leaned back in the leather passenger seat of the BMW 720 and smiled. Another good day. Fifty kilos and he didn't have to kill anyone for it. Not that he minded killing. It was simply a part of the business. Plus, he was good at it. He hadn't gotten the nickname *Mozo* for being squeamish about taking lives.

"Where to?" the driver, Tito Escobar asked in perfect English. In the back seat two other gangsters chattered loudly.

Morales closed his eyes and thought for a moment. "The warehouse," he finally said. "We don't need to be caught rolling with fifty keys in the trunk and I don't want to keep it at the house anymore. Besides, we've got some other business to take care of."

Escobar nodded and pointed the car toward the north end of Las Vegas Boulevard.

Outside, the Strip was alive with the sights and sounds of Las Vegas, at least the Las Vegas depicted in the movies. Drunken revelers stumbling from casino to casino; neon lights and gaudy reconstructions of foreign cities and historic monuments; and, of course, the requisite stands advertising sex for sale dotting every corner. This place wasn't called "Sin City" for nothing. No fantasy was out of bounds, no vice unattainable.

For Gluttony, you could indulge in the pandemic of all-you-can-eat buffets. For Greed you could fritter away your life savings chasing the elusive jackpots advertised by the casinos. Sins of the flesh could be satiated by punching up an 800 number on your telephone. Within ten minutes a woman would be at your hotel door ready to take your money for a few minutes of pleasure. And if you wanted a little white powder to go with your four-day party you could get that too.

That's where Miguel Morales came in.

As leader of the Mexican Mafia in Nevada it was his job to make sure that chemicals were readily available to anyone who wanted them. It was simple economics—the law of supply and demand. He had the supply for those who had the demand.

He wasn't the typical gangster. In fact, he saw himself as a businessman, more along the lines of Donald Trump or Bill Gates. He was just like them in one important way: he provided a product that was in demand. It was that simple. And the fact that his product could be acquired only via illegal means was even better. The war on drugs in America had been the best thing for his business. It basically created the black market that kept prices inflated and kept him swimming in tax-free cash. He cringed every time he heard people talking about legalizing drugs. That would be the worst thing that could happen to his business.

Granted, *La eMe* was diversified. Drugs were big, but they weren't the gang's only business. Hookers, guns, robbery, identity theft. There was nothing they wouldn't try; nothing they couldn't do. America was the land of opportunity for criminals too.

• • •

At the warehouse Morales held the gun to the back of the informant's head and pulled the trigger. Jaime Mota, bound, gagged, and on his knees, fell forward in a puddle of his own blood and brains.

Morales turned and faced the rest of his leadership. "That's how we deal with rats. Any questions?"

There were none.

"Good, now let's get some food. My treat."

• • •

Over dinner at Pizza Shack Morales and three of his lieutenants communicated in code. Everything related to gang business was talked about cryptically. You never knew when someone was going to be listening in, especially the feds.

"The Lakers won by two last night," Morales said to the group.

Translation: *Two kilos are coming in from Los Angeles.*

"When do they play next?" Cholo Vasquez asked.

When will they be here?

"I'll have to check the schedule for this week," Morales replied.

Sometime this week.

"Who's starting the next game?" Tito Escobar asked the question this time.

Who do you want to make the pick up?

"Probably the usual lineup," Morales answered. "They're the most reliable."

The three of you.

"What about the Padres? How have they been doing?" Felipe Jones piped in. He was the only high-ranking member of *La eMe* in Nevada who hadn't been born in Mexico. His mother had come to Las Vegas from Matamoros years earlier and married his father, a *gringo*.

What about the shipment of guns coming from San Diego?

Morales nodded. "They're on the road for two games. I think they're going with the usual lineup too."

They will be here in two days. Same guys make the pickup.

"Hi guys," the waiter interrupted as he slid two trays of pizza on top of the table. "Looks like we've got one sausage and one pepperoni." He set a stack of plates and napkins next to the pizzas and wiped his hands on a yellowed apron cinched around his waist. "Can I get you anything else?"

Morales shook his head. "We're good. Thanks."

"All right. My name is Justin. If you need anything just let me know."The waiter smiled and turned and left.

Morales quickly gobbled up three slices of pepperoni and then went to work scribbling on a yellow notepad. When he was done he ripped off the top page and handed it to Tito Escobar who read it and nodded.

"Understood?" Morales asked.

"Understood," Escobar replied, and then went back to his pizza.

30

The Walleye Mafia

"Man, those guys freak me out." Justin Warner spoke softly in the kitchen. He didn't want the Mexicans to hear him.

"How come?" Jace Caldwell asked. "They seem harmless enough."

Justin glanced curiously at the pizza cook. "Man, do you know who those guys are? I mean, do you have any freaking idea?"

Caldwell peeked around the corner at the group of Mexicans and then pulled his head back. "They look like a bunch of illegals. Probably doing some roofing job around here."

Justin pulled the cook farther back into the kitchen behind the pizza oven. "Don't say that kind of shit," he cautioned. "You don't want to mess with those guys."

"Why not? Who are they?"

"*La eMe*," the waiter mumbled.

"La who?"

"*La eMe*," Warner repeated. "The Mexican Mafia."

"Mexican Mafia?" Caldwell looked at Warner and laughed. "You mean like *The Godfather* only the Mexican version?"

"Shut up," Warner cautioned the cook. "Yes, that's what I mean. You've never heard of them?"

Caldwell shook his head. "Sorry, dude. Remember, I'm not from around here."

"Oh, yeah, I forgot. Where are you from again?"

It seemed everyone in Las Vegas was from somewhere else originally.

"Ely, Minnesota," Caldwell replied.

"I guess you don't have the Mexican Mafia up there, huh?"

"We don't have the Mexican Mafia, Italian Mafia, or Bohemian Mafia. No Mafia in Ely. Wait, I take that back. We have the Walleye Mafia. They're a ruthless gang of fishermen. They're nasty. Fuck you up and steal all your fish." He laughed at his own joke.

"You're an idiot," Warner muttered.

"That's what I'm told," Caldwell replied. "Anyway, so what's the deal with these guys?"

Warner gave him the CliffsNotes version of the Mexican Mafia and their recent activities in and around Las Vegas. Murder, extortion, drugs, bodies buried out in the desert. *Lots* of bodies.

"And these four wetbacks are all part of this?"

Warner nodded slowly, and then added, "Don't call them wetbacks."

"OK, then, spiks."

"You know, I'm half Mexican."

"Which half? The bad half?"

Caldwell laughed again at his own wittiness. Warner didn't join him.

"Man, screw you," the waiter said and turned to walk away. "You're hopeless."

"Hey, wait," Caldwell said, snagging Warner by the arm. "Look, I'm sorry. I was just joking around. Sometimes I take things too far. I guess I did that just now."

Warner eyed him warily.

"Look," the cook continued, "I mean it. I'm sorry. No more Mexican jokes."

"I don't care about the Mexican jokes. I care about those guys out there hearing any of this."

"You worry too much, dude. What are they going to do, shoot us?"

"Maybe."

"Hey, Jace? Justin?" Anette Bonilla's shrill voice came from the front near the cash register.

Both men stepped from behind the stainless steel oven.

"Yeah, we're back here," Jace called to her.

"What are you guys doing?" the cashier asked.

"Uh, nothing," Justin answered. "Just talking."

Anette's hands went to her shapely hips. "Well, talk later. I've got two orders to fill. Large garbage pizza and a deep dish Chicago. *Comprende?*"

"*Comprende, mamacita.*" Caldwell saluted and grinned broadly.

The harsh look stamped on her face softened and she smiled. "Your Spanish is getting better. Are you ready for some private tutoring?" A playful smirk followed by a wink.

"Are you offering your services, *chica?*" Caldwell chuckled mischievously.

"Perhaps."

Justin stepped between the two and raised his hands. "OK, you two, that's enough. You're making me sick."

Caldwell slapped the waiter on the back and stepped around him making his way to the door. "You're just jealous, dude. Jealous 'cuz our lovely cashier here digs me and not you."

Now, Justin laughed. "Hello, idiot, I'm not jealous. I'm gay, remember? If anything, I'd pick you over her." He glanced over his shoulder. "Sorry, Anette, no offense."

"My loss," the cashier pouted playfully. "Anyway, can you get moving on those pizzas, babe? We can discuss your private lessons later."

"So are you saying you dig me?" Caldwell winked at Warner.

"Oh, Jesus," the waiter muttered. "How about we drop this whole thing, OK?"

"Hey, consider it dropped, dude." Caldwell made his way to the oven and rolled out a sheet of pizza dough. "I've got work to do anyway, and so do you. You'd better go check on the Corleone family out there before they bury you in the desert too."

• • •

He found it after they'd closed the restaurant and locked the front door. It was beneath the table where the *La eMe* gangsters had dined, wedged between the vinyl base of the booth and the carpeted floor. He dislodged the item as he ran the vacuum cleaner beneath the table.

"Holy shit," he muttered under his breath as he retrieved the roll of tightly wrapped hundred dollar bills from the floor.

"What?" Anette said from behind the cash register as she scribbled the day's take in a battered ledger.

At first he didn't speak, couldn't speak. It was as if all the air had been sucked out of his lungs. Then, he managed to say, "Look," as he held up the money roll.

Anette maneuvered through the maze of tables and took the money in her hands. "My God, where did you find that?"

Justin pointed beneath the table.

"How…I mean, who's is it?"

One word, mumbled slowly, almost reverently. "*La eMe*."

"Hey, what's going on out here?" Caldwell said as he came over and stood next to them. His eyes grew wide once he caught a glimpse of the money roll. "Dude, that's some tip they left you."

Justin shot the cook a dirty look. "It's not a tip. I found it under the table. They must have lost it."

"Well, you know the old saying: finders keepers. Man, how much do you think is in there?"

"I don't know," Justin shrugged.

"What are you waiting for, dude? Let's count it."

Justin undid the rubber band that held the roll together and peeled the bills apart one at a time laying them gingerly on the tabletop. Ninety one-hundred-dollar bills.

"That's nine thousand bones," Caldwell noted. "Three grand each if we split it evenly."

Justin looked back over his shoulder. "We're not splitting this."

"Fine," Caldwell said angrily. "Keep it all yourself. Be greedy. Don't share with your friends."

"That's not what I meant. We're not keeping this money. It's not ours. It belongs to those gangsters."

"Maybe we should turn it in to the police," Anette interjected.

"Are you crazy?" Caldwell sputtered. "This is like a gift from heaven. Like when the Jews were wandering in the desert and God made it rain pizza."

"It was manna," Justin said as he rolled his eyes, "not pizza. And it's not a gift because we're not going to keep it."

"Really? I thought it was pizza. What the hell is manna?"

"You can Google it later," Anette said. "Let's figure out what we're going to do with this money."

"Manna, hmm," Caldwell mumbled softly as he scratched his chin. "Could have sworn it was pizza."

• • •

The decision had been made: they would split the money three ways. Justin finally caved after being convinced that the gangsters probably had no idea where they'd actually lost the money. *Probably*. The word tugged at the back of his mind. The more he thought about it, though, the more it made sense. They didn't know where the money was, and there was no way they'd ever report nine thousand dollars in lost drug profits to the police. Maybe Jace was right; perhaps it was manna from heaven. Or pizza from heaven, in his case.

"Do you guys want to grab a drink somewhere?" Jace posed the question as they stood on the darkened front stoop while Anette locked the front door. "I'll buy."

Justin was about to reply when two strong beams of light raked across the parking lot and the front of the Pizza Shack. He froze in the halogen glare. The gangsters were back looking for their money and probably pissed. The car screeched to a cockeyed halt in front of where they stood and a man jumped out, wild-eyed and agitated. His ragged hair stood up on end, giving him the appearance of a feral jungle beast.

"Hey, you still open?" he mumbled. "I wanna order a pizza."

Justin breathed a sigh of relief. "No, we're closed. We closed an hour ago."

"Then what the fuck you still doing here?"

"Well, we had to clean up…"

"Fuck that shit," the jungle man spat out. "I'm hungry. Get back in there and make me a fucking pizza. Canadian bacon and olives."

"Dude, we're closed. Get your drunk ass out of here."

"Man, fuck you." His words slurred together: *Mangfushyou*. He took a menacing step toward the group but tripped over a concrete divider. Arms flailing, he righted himself before hitting the ground.

"Come on, guys, let's get out of here," Anette said. As an afterthought she turned toward the jungle man and pointed to the east. "If you're that hungry there's a McDonald's half a mile from here."

The jungle man started to curse, but stopped. "Man…" His words trailed off. He stopped, looked at all of them with glassy, bloodshot eyes and turned and stumbled back behind the wheel. As he tore out of the parking lot maniacal laughter floated from inside his car. None of them saw the small boy in the back seat though.

31

Halfway to Henderson

Halfway to Henderson six-year-old Tommy Foster stirred in the back seat. He'd been dreaming about pizza for some reason. As he rubbed the sleep from his eyes he glanced around his surroundings; he was in the backseat of his dad's car again, the exhaust humming loudly from behind him. On the seat next to him sat his best friend, goofy grin permanently stitched across his yellow face. Tommy smiled. "Hi, SpongeBob," he whispered into the stuffed toy's ear. "Did you sleep good?"

In the boy's mind his yellow friend answered. "*I sure did, Tommy.*"

"I'm glad. Did you have any cool dreams?"

SpongeBob prefaced his answer with his trademark cackle. Then he said, "*I dreamt that I was a giant pizza.*"

"Hey, I dreamt about pizza too," the boy said.

SpongeBob didn't reply, though. Instead, a gruff blob of slurred words floated over the headrest.

"Are you talking to that goddamn stuffed animal again?"

His father's voice quieted the boy. He pulled *SpongeBob* close to his chest and buried his face in the soft fabric.

"Answer me, boy."

"Yes, sir," Tommy answered meekly.

Tommy Foster Sr. reached over the seat and swatted at his son. He hit nothing but air as the boy scrambled to the other side of the car out of the way. "You're a quick little fucking monkey," the man snarled from the front.

The boy burrowed into a pile of trash: empty beer cans, hamburger wrappers, and miscellaneous junk.

His father laughed again, more sinister this time. "Go ahead, hide in the pile of shit. Once we stop, I'll get you."

I wish he would just go away. It wasn't the first time he'd had that thought. In fact, that sentiment popped into his head several times a day. Maybe then someone would find him a home with parents who loved him. Maybe they'd have kids too; brothers with whom he could play LEGOs and baseball and throw a football around. A real family, not a drunk father and a mother who…well, he didn't actually know where his mother was. She'd been gone awhile.

Suddenly, the car lurched violently over the center line. The drunk behind the wheel cursed and cranked the steering wheel hard to the right, overcorrecting the swerving vehicle. A moment later he regained control of the car and eased up on the gas pedal.

"See what you made me do," the boy's father screamed. "I almost lost control because of you."

"I didn't do anyth…" A harsh slap across his face cut the word in half. He scrambled to the other side of the car, behind the driver's seat, and bit down hard on his tears. He wasn't going to cry—wasn't going to let the drunk know he'd hurt him again.

"Shut up! Don't give me no lip. I'm your father."

He wanted to scream back. *You're a crummy father and I wish you were dead!* But he didn't. Instead, he nursed his cut lip by holding it between his fingers.

"*Everything's going to be OK, Tommy.*" It was SpongeBob, his voice soothing, calm. "*I won't let anything bad happen to you.*"

32

The Shaved Kitten

He never really wanted to be a father. That was never in his plans. Then, the bitch had to go and get herself pregnant. It was all her fault. He told her that too, many times, as he slapped her around their tiny apartment in the shadow of the Strip. She'd told him she was on the pill. Had he known the sniveling little shit in the back seat would be the product of their coupling he never would have banged the bitch. Instead of living the high life like a twenty-four-year old should he was stuck babysitting this *thing* in the back seat who thought his stuffed toy was real.

God, he wished she would have gotten an abortion. He tried convincing her but every time he brought it up she said no. Some shit about it being wrong. He should have just taken a coat hanger and scrambled the kid himself. The thought made him laugh. Scrambled kid. That was funny. Then, an idea blossomed in the back of his alcohol-soaked mind. Why not? Who would miss the little punk? Plus, the desert out here was huge. The more he thought about it the more he liked the idea. Complete freedom was a hole in the desert away. It wouldn't even have to be a deep hole—a couple feet, maybe. Whatever didn't stay buried would be eaten in a matter of hours by the desert scavengers. No one would ever have to know. He'd pack up all his shit and hit the road. Maybe finally head to LA and get started on his acting career. He was destined for stardom; he'd always believed that. As far as he was concerned, he was the next Brad Pitt. Then the stain in the back seat came along and ruined everything. But now...

His murderous train of thought derailed at the sight of the flashing neon sign just past the freeway overpass: The Shaved Kitten, his favorite strip joint. The women there were the hottest around. Plus, they went the extra mile if you paid them enough.

He slid the '79 Cadillac Eldorado between two semis at the back of the lot, jammed it into park, and killed the ignition. "Stay in here," he snarled as he looked into the backseat at his son. "If you so much as make a sound I'll snap you in half." *Who knows, I might just do that anyway*, he thought.

The boy dropped his eyes to the garbage-covered floorboard and nodded, cowed.

Before locking the door Tommy Sr. poked his head back inside the car. "And quit talking to that goddamn stuffed toy."

• • •

The call came in shortly after midnight.

"Squad three-ten."

"Go ahead."

A pause from the other end of the police radio punctuated by the click-clack of furious typing in the background. "Three-ten," the 911 dispatcher finally said through a haze of static, "I need you to check on a child locked in a grey Cadillac in the parking lot of *The Shaved Kitten*. White male, five to eight years old. Caller says the kid's been there for an hour or so."

Officer Jack Martin depressed the button on the side of the microphone. "Copy that."

Leaving your kid in the car at The Shaved Kitten. That was new. Not that he was surprised. After ten years on the job nothing surprised him anymore. Even what some people did to their kids. Still, he'd never had a call like this before.

"What's wrong with people?" The question came from Leon Roberts behind the wheel.

Martin shook his head sadly. "I don't know. Some people just shouldn't have kids."

Roberts nodded in agreement. "Isn't that true. You know, you need a license to do just about anything else: drive a car, open a business, hell, even catch fish. But for the most important job in the world you don't need anything."

"Is this your 'more people should be neutered' speech?"

Roberts' husky laugh echoed through the squad. "You've heard it before?"

"Yeah, only about a dozen times."

"I'll shut up then," Roberts said as he smiled. "What should we talk about?"

"How about normal guy stuff? Football. Baseball. Women."

"Ha," Roberts spat out. "Don't get me started on women."

Martin rolled his eyes. "Leon, who are you kidding? You're married to the nicest woman in the world. What the hell do you have to complain about?"

A sheepish grin from the former UNLV basketball star. "I know," he muttered. "Macy is a hell of a wife."

Roberts guided the marked squad car onto a frontage road and through a four-way stop. As they crested a small rise, the gaudy neon sign of The Shaved Kitten peeked over the darkened horizon. They'd both been to this joint many times, not as patrons but for work. Both cops knew one immutable fact: booze and naked women were a breeding ground for trouble. As they pulled into the parking lot Martin told the dispatcher of their arrival. She copied their transmission and noted the time.

"There it is," Martin said, pointing to the Eldorado sandwiched between the two semis. He activated the spotlight, directing the high-powered beam on the vehicle.

"Looks like a white-trash mobile," Roberts said.

Martin laughed. "What else would it be at this joint? Certainly not one of your brothers."

Roberts shot his partner a baleful glare, and then smiled. "You're right. The brothers would be hanging out at Mousey's."

"Another fine establishment for adult entertainment," Martin joked.

"Those dancers, the way they snake down those poles and do the splits, they're artists."

"Hey, how often do you think they clean those poles?" Roberts asked. "I mean, it has to get kind of…slimy."

"Nasty," Martin smirked. "If we never had another call in one of these joints I couldn't be happier. Everything about them is scuzzy. The women, the patrons. The owners too."

"Yeah, they're the worst," Roberts agreed. "What's the guy's name who owns this place?"

"Jerry Danglewood," Martin answered. "He used to produce porno movies out in LA. I think he did *No Holes Barred* and *Queefe Party*."

"Classy," Roberts muttered under his breath. "How do you know all this crap?"

Martin shrugged. "Remember, I used to work vice. Learned way too much about hookers and the porn business."

"Didn't you have to do undercover work in some gay bathhouses too?"

Martin nodded. "Yeah. I've blocked all that shit out of my mind though." He paused for a moment, and then added, "That place ruined my whole opinion of Crisco."

• • •

The boy was scared. The nervous, uncertain look in his eyes told them that much. Simply getting his name had been like pulling teeth. But, after a few minutes of cajoling and talking about SpongeBob, the boy spilled everything. His name, dad's name, and everything else that had transpired over the past two hours on their journey to The Shaved Kitten.

Ten minutes later, with the boy safely ensconced in the back of squad 310, Martin and Roberts dragged the boy's handcuffed father out of *The Shaved Kitten* kicking and screaming. A crowd of onlookers had gathered around the scene, drawn by the drunk's incoherent wailing. Another squad arrived at the scene. Martin opened the rear door and Roberts shoved Tommy Foster Sr. into the backseat. After the door slammed, the drunk threw himself against the barred windows, screaming loudly and frothing at the mouth.

"Nice guy," Roberts commented as he joined Martin and Tracy Marx at the front of the car.

"Yeah, he's a real peach," Officer Marx commented. "Is he single? I'm in the market."

"Whoa," Martin said. "You'll have to get in line. I want to set him up with my sister."

The three cops laughed loudly.

After their laughter subsided Martin glanced over his shoulder. "What about the kid?"

"Well, I suppose we should take him to St. Mike's," Roberts said. "Mom is in jail and there's no one else around to take care of him."

"Yeah, that makes the most sense," Marx offered. "I'll book this guy for child neglect."

"Thanks," Martin said.

Marx shrugged. "It'll give me a chance to get to know him better." She smiled and got behind the wheel of her cruiser. A minute later she was gone, the drunk still screaming loudly and kicking at the barred windows.

"What an asshole," Roberts muttered.

"Who, me?"

"Yeah, you, Jack."

Martin laughed again. "Come on, buddy, let's get this kid to St. Mike's. I'll call Hope Stannes at the Department of Child Welfare and leave her a message so she can look into this kid's case first thing in the morning."

●　●　●

Two blocks from St. Michael's Home for Children Tommy Foster asked what there was to do there.

Martin turned and looked over his shoulder. "All kinds of things, kiddo. Games, books, movies."

"Movies? Really?"

Martin nodded.

"What kind?" the boy asked.

Roberts chimed in this time. "You name it and they've got it, little man. *The Lion King, Finding Nemo, Snow White*."

Tommy sat up and pressed his chin against the back of the seat. "*Snow White?*"

"Uh-huh," Roberts nodded.

"Fuck that," the six-year-old replied matter-of-factly as he sat back in the seat and grinned. "I wanna watch SpongeBob."

33

Holding out Hope

Hope Stannes punched up her voice mail. Jack Martin's voice greeted her. As he spoke she scribbled on a yellow legal pad on top of her desk, overgrown with a thicket of paperwork, books and notepads. *Tommy Foster. St. Mike's. Father, Tommy Foster Sr., booked for child neglect.* Martin's message came to a close and she finished writing with a flourish. Two minutes later she was on the line with St. Mike's scrawling more notes, this time in the blue-lined margins of the notepad.

"I'll be there by nine," Hope informed the intake coordinator on the other end of the line.

"Fine by me," the young woman said curtly and hung up.

Hope grabbed the notepad and slid it into her briefcase along with a stack of new release forms. It seemed the county was always changing the paperwork, as well as the subsequent rules that governed the paperwork. As far as she was concerned, half the stuff she filled out on a daily basis was unnecessary. All it did was keep the folks in the paperwork division on the state payroll.

In the hallway outside her office she locked the door behind her. There had been some problems lately with thefts in the building. They weren't sure if it was someone from the outside who'd wandered in, or if the perpetrator was an employee. Swift retribution and punishment had been promised by county officials via an e-mailed memo last week though. She had no doubt they'd catch the thief; video cameras stared down at them from every corner through opaque, lifeless eyes that monitored virtually every living thing in the building. She'd even heard that a young couple in accounting had been caught in an amorous embrace in one of the supply closets last month. After hearing that, she cheered for the young lovers. At least someone was getting some.

Halfway down the hallway she passed two colleagues and nodded and smiled. A few more paces and she stood at the stainless steel elevator doors. She was jonesing for a coffee, black with a shot of espresso dumped in for good measure. She'd hit The Magic Bean on the way to St. Mike's. If she skipped her daily caffeine infusion she'd have a splitting headache by noon.

"What do you know about this Tommy Foster case?" The husky voice came from behind her.

She whirled around and saw her boss standing there. George Sampson stood a full foot taller than she and was built like an oak tree. A former offensive tackle with the Washington Redskins, Sampson had landed his job with Child Welfare after blowing his knee out five years earlier during a game with the Chicago Bears.

"No 'good morning' today?" Hope queried playfully.

Sampson looked down at her and then smiled. "Sorry. Good morning, Hope. How are you this lovely morning?"

Hope laughed. "Fine. And I don't know much about Foster yet. I'm on my way to St. Mike's right now to meet the kid."

"Good. Let me know once you talk with the boy."

The request was unusual. Sampson never asked to know about a case unless there were some extenuating circumstances.

"Sure," she replied. "Can I ask why? Seems like a pretty routine case."

Sampson nodded gravely. "Yeah, I guess it would be except for one thing: the kid's dad died in police custody last night. Something about alcohol poisoning and acute cocaine psychosis."

．　．　．

Hope found the boy playing with LEGOs by himself in the far corner of the toy room. He was a cutie. Sandy-brown hair that hung in wispy ropes past his ears and over his forehead. It was his eyes she found the most intriguing, however; dark, expressive orbs behind which she knew lurked a lifetime of knotted hurt. Damage that would probably take years of therapy to unravel.

As she entered the room Tommy Foster looked back at her. She smiled but his face remained neutral.

"Hi, Tommy." She knelt down next to the boy. "My name is Hope."

The uncertain, wary look on his face deepened and she wondered if he'd talk with her at all. In his report from last night, Officer

Martin indicated that the boy had been quiet at first, but then after a while had opened up. Hopefully, that would happen here today. She didn't want him going completely catatonic. She'd seen that before with severely abused children. That was perhaps the hardest part of her job. Children so damaged that they were realistically beyond all hope. She didn't like thinking that anyone was beyond hope, but sometimes that was simply the harsh reality of things.

"I'm here to talk with you about what happened last night," she continued.

"You mean with my dad?" His voice was soft, almost birdlike.

She nodded, surprised at how quickly he'd spoken. Part of her wasn't sure he'd speak at all today.

"Yes, that's why I'm here. And I also have some bad news."

As the last words sunk in, his face took on a stern, impassive look. She got the distinct impression that he was accustomed to hearing bad news.

"Is my dad OK?"

Nervous, she stood and pulled a chair next to the boy. This was the part she hated most about her job. Death notifications were never good, but someone had to be the bearer of bad news. Unfortunately, that task usually fell on her shoulders.

"Yes, it's about your dad," she said, nodding. "He died at the jail last night."

What happened next took her completely by surprise. Instead of going catatonic or breaking down, the boy brightened, a broad grin spreading across his freckled face.

"Really? That's great!"

She was taken aback. In all her years as a child abuse case worker she'd never experienced something like this. Even with the most acutely abused kids. The death of a parent, no matter how abusive, was traumatic for children. At least it was supposed to be.

"I thought you'd be sad," Hope commented, trying to keep the judgment out of her voice. He was only six, after all.

Tommy shook his head vigorously. "Nu-uh. Dad was a mean man and he hit me a lot. Now he won't be doing that anymore. And I won't have to sit in the car anymore when he goes to those places where the ladies take their clothes off. Or the casino."

Her heart almost broke. The words came out so effortlessly, so innocently. Six years old, she thought, and this little boy had probably experienced more heartbreak and abuse than most people would encounter in a lifetime.

"Plus," the boy continued, "SpongeBob said everything was going to be OK and that he'd keep me safe." He held up his stuffed toy.

"Really? SpongeBob said all that."

The boy nodded. "Can you find me a family now? One with a mom and dad and two brothers."

This time, she laughed. "I'll see what I can do." She didn't stop smiling until she was behind the wheel of her car. Then, she had an unorthodox idea.

• • •

"I really think we could do this," Hope spoke excitedly into her cell phone. "I know it sounds a little crazy, but I know we could make it work."

"A little crazy," her husband laughed on the other end of the line. "Honey, it's more than a little crazy."

"Why?" Her tone was sharp, determined.

"Well…I don't know…just because it is. We don't know anything about this kid. He could be a little psychopath. Burn the house down, kill the cat. That kind of stuff."

"We don't even have a cat," Hope retorted. After a short pause she added snidely, "And we'll keep all the matches under lock and key until we know for sure he's not a psycho."

"Hope, honey, look, we just can't…"

"…'go around adopting every homeless kid you come in contact with at work'," she parroted his words from previous conversations. "Look, I know, and in all fairness, I haven't brought it up for the past two years. Not since that little Cuban girl whose parents drowned trying to get here."

"Yeah, I know," Andrew Stannes conceded.

"Besides," Hope continued, "I'm not talking about adoption right away. We could have him as a foster child and if things work out then maybe consider adoption. That's how it usually works."

Silence from the other end of the line. She wasn't sure if she'd successfully talked him into it or if he had just tuned her out. Then, "How about we talk about it tonight?"

She smiled. "That's all I'm asking for. Let's talk about it and see if it will work for us. We both know having kids of our own is never going to happen."

As soon as the words escaped her lips she regretted saying them. They'd been to countless fertility specialists over the years trying to determine why they could never get pregnant. Dr. Franz Mohrbacher finally gave them their answer late last year: Andrew was sterile. Since then they had mulled over the idea of adopting, always backing out at the last minute, hoping beyond hope for an immaculate conception.

"Don't remind me," Andrew muttered sullenly.

"I'm sorry," Hope said. "You know what I mean though. And why not Tommy? He literally has no one. If we don't step up he's going to be placed into the state system and who knows where he'll end up, or what kind of people he'll end up with."

"But we'll talk about it first, right? Before you get your hopes up?"

"Yes," she said. "I promise. If, after talking about it, we don't both agree that it will work for us, then we don't do it. All I want to do right now is look at it as a possibility."

"Deal. When will you be home?"

"Should be a bit after three," she said as she glanced at her watch. "First, I have to stop at Toys"R"Us and pick up a bunch of stuff for Tommy's new room."

A mischievous laugh and she was gone before he could reply.

34

Count Crapula

George Sampson had spent much of the day dealing with the Tommy Foster case. It wasn't every day that a drunken, drug addict father left his child in the car at a strip joint and then had the audacity to die in jail. The compassionate part of him thought it was a tragedy; the jaded part thought the kid was probably going to be better for it. Usually, the jaded part was right.

He hadn't always been this callous. Before entering the child abuse trenches he actually held out hope for humanity. Not anymore. In his opinion, Freud's observations on human behavior had been right: people were garbage.

If only his knee hadn't given out in that game against the Bears all those years ago. Maybe then he'd have a better opinion of humanity. Then again, maybe not. The world of professional football hadn't been populated by saints either. There was just as much alcoholism, drug abuse, and depravity on an NFL football team as there was behind closed doors in the ghetto or trailer parks of America.

Probably more, in fact, due to the obscene amounts of money pro football players made.

He supposed much of it was due to uncorrected human nature. Most "decent" people grew up with parents who taught them right from wrong and imposed consequences for deviating from the correct path. A lot of pro football players came from broken homes and grew up in an environment where their athletic ability could get them out of any jam. Consequently, accountability was something foreign to them. Just like Tommy Foster Sr., more than likely. The man had been twenty-four. That meant he fathered Tommy Jr. at eighteen. Way too young to be a parent, as far as he was concerned. Christ, knowing what he knew now about raising his own three children, thirty was too young. Maybe even forty.

As Sampson sat behind his computer a new e-mail popped up on the screen. It was from Hope. He skimmed the memo once and then reread it. He was about to dial her number when his phone rang. Caller ID said it was his brother in Austin.

"You crafty brother," Sampson proclaimed as he picked up the phone, "they said you were hung."

From twelve hundred miles away Irvin Sampson finished the sequence. "They were right about that."

Both men erupted in riotous laughter. The edited bit was from *Blazing Saddles*. Despite the film's liberal use of the "n" word it was still one of their all-time favorite movies.

"So, what's up?" George asked his younger brother. "How are things in the music biz?"

"Man, don't get me started."

Irvin Sampson had started Cowboy Records in Austin, Texas, to capitalize on the lack of black country music recording artists. To date, he'd had one client, a former Crip gang member straight out of Compton, California, who tried melding country music and rap. Count Crapula never made it off the ground. In fact, he made it into the ground, six feet under following a drive-by in Long Beach.

"Hey, hang in there," George said encouragingly. "It's all going to work out for you."

"Yeah, when?" the younger Sampson snorted. "It's been almost two years and I've got nothing to show for it."

"Hey, if it wasn't for you the world would have never heard of Count Chocula."

Irvin sighed. "Count Crapula," he corrected his brother.

"Oh, right. Well, whatever. It's going to happen someday. I know it, bro."

"Maybe I should just stick to rap like all the other brothers and give up this black country thing."

"Do you want my opinion?" George asked.

"Do I have a choice?"

George chuckled gruffly. He'd never been shy about giving his opinion whether people wanted to hear it or not. "I think you should do whatever makes you happy," he said. "If it's country music you want to do, then do it. But…"

"Here it comes," Irvin interrupted.

"Wait, hang on a sec," George said, a touch of anger in his voice. "You didn't even let me finish what I was going to say."

"OK, I'm sorry."

"Forget about it. What I was going to say was this: do you think maybe you're limiting yourself too much?"

"What do you mean?" Irvin queried.

"Well, maybe you should look at expanding beyond just black country music stars. Seems like kind of a limited pool of talent. If your thing is country music, why not look for the best, most talented artists, period. Forget about their race."

"Yeah," Irvin muttered after a short silence. "I've actually thought about that. Especially after that whole Count Crapula disaster."

Laughter from the Nevada end of the line. "That was a mess," George said. "That cat, he was straight-up ghetto 'hood rat."

It was Irvin's turn to laugh, and he did it with gusto. "Yeah, I know. I thought we had something, though. Country and rap."

"Maybe, but I don't know if all your redneck brethren out there would have gone for it."

"Hey, wait a minute," Irvin retorted. "It's not just rednecks who are into country. There's a lot of us brownnecks out there who like it too."

"I know, I was just kidding," George replied.

"Anyway, what's new with you?" Irvin asked, shifting the subject.

George filled him in on his life in southern Nevada. Work was busy, but good. Kids were occupied with school and sports and Louisa was thinking about retiring from the school district. "When are you going to come out here again?"

"Soon," Irvin said. "In fact, I've been thinking about moving out there if things don't work out for me in the music business. I've been looking into casino security and think I'd like doing something like that."

"Plenty of jobs out here," George added. "Not a bad idea, bro. For your sake, though, I hope you never have to move out here."

"Why's that?" The surprise in Irvin's voice was obvious.

After a short pause George finally spoke. "Because it would mean your dreams didn't come true," he explained. "And believe me, I know what it's like to have your dreams taken away from you."

"That's pretty deep," Irvin replied.

"Deep or not, I hope it all works out for you. You deserve it." Then, he added, "What are you up to this weekend? Want to fly out and hit the strip? Louisa is gone for her girls weekend and the kids are busy doing whatever they do with their friends."

"Man, I'd love to, but I can't," Irvin explained. "I'm supposed to go and see this guy play at some dive bar downtown. Joby Kidd. He sent me an e-mail a couple weeks ago so I thought I'd go and check him out. He can't be any worse than Count Crapula."

George's laughter turned into a minor coughing fit. After re-gaining his voice he said, "No problem. Maybe this Joby Kidd will finally put Cowboy Records on the map."

Irvin sighed loudly. "I hope so. 'Cuz if this doesn't pan out, I'm done with the music biz altogether."

Austin

35

In It for Better

The Dream.

That's what he'd called his chase for country music fame and fortune all these years. Only it hadn't been just his dream; it was *theirs*. At least it had been until yesterday. Had he not been three sheets to the wind now, the irony might have elicited a laugh. After all these years of writing songs about cheating wives, drunken dogs, and pickup trucks he had finally become a caricature of his own music.

Joby Kidd sat alone at the bar mindlessly popping stale peanuts into his mouth and nursing a half-consumed beer. From the archaic jukebox in the corner George Jones' plaintive wail filled the hazy, smoke-clogged air. Just another night in Austin, he thought. Only now, he was on the losing end of a country song, and his soon-to-be ex-wife was on her way to Hollywood to finally make it big. Or, more likely, find someone else who'd already made it big.

It hadn't always been like this. Once, there had been hope for a rhinestone-studded future of hit songs, sold-out concerts, a fleet of expensive cars and a luxurious mansion on a hill. Back then, two years gone, he'd told Becky that his star was on the rise and that she'd be wise to hitch her wagon to it now while the getting was good. She must have believed him. Three months after their first date they were married by the justice of the peace in San Antonio. She got a job working as a waitress at a truck stop while he found work changing oil at the local Speedy Lube. That was how he spent his days. Nights were different, though, consisting of putting lyrics to music in their tiny apartment, or performing for bleary-eyed patrons in seedy dive bars in the underbelly of town. He didn't play in those bars for the money; he did it for the experience and the exposure. He called it *Paying My Dues*, and had even written a song about it. All great artists had to have at least one song chronicling how difficult their climb to the top of the charts had been.

Joby removed the battered cowboy hat from his head and ran a hand through his dark locks before downing the rest of his beer. The hat had been with him through thick and thin since his foray into country music began five years earlier. It had been more loyal than his wife. The thought made him laugh.

"Ready for another, Joby?" Sam Houston asked from behind the bar as he ran a towel through a damp mug.

The singer nodded. "Why not?"

The mustachioed bartender topped off a fresh mug with a frothy head of Budweiser and slid it down the bar.

"Thanks."

Houston nodded and went back to drying beer mugs and masticating the large wad of chaw jammed into his cheeks. After a few moments of silence he spoke. "You gonna be OK?"

Joby looked up from his beer and shrugged. "What choice to I have? I don't plan on killing myself over her."

The bartender nodded slowly, thoughtfully. "Good. No woman's worth that."

"Yeah…I guess."

Houston marched to the end of the bar and quickly filled an order. He returned a few moments later, towel slung over his shoulder. He propped his elbows on the scuffed bartop and hunched his shoulders. "How'd she do it?" he asked. "Let you know she was leaving, I mean."

Joby looked up at the bartender. He reached into his pocket and pulled out a sheet of notebook paper with ragged edges. He slapped the note down hard. Houston took it and read the hastily scribbled note slowly, seeming to savor every word. When he was done he folded the note and gently handed it back to Joby.

"That's harsh," he muttered.

"Tell me about it. I found it on the kitchen table this morning."

Houston leaned over behind the bar and expelled the dark wad of chew into a wastebasket. It landed with a dull thud in the bottom of the container.

"Seems to me like she was nothing but a gold digger," Houston mused. "Women like that, they don't stick around long. If they don't get what they want right away they're off to find someone who can provide it for them."

Joby nodded absently. The bartender was right; he could see that now. But two years ago...well, he thought she'd really loved him.

"You know what," Joby muttered after a short stretch of silence.

"What's that?"

The singer gulped down a large swig of beer and wiped his lips on the back of his sleeve. A low burp escaped his mouth. "I really loved her," he explained. "I really did. Would have done anything for her."

Houston's head bobbed sagely. "Doesn't matter how much you loved her," he said. "She didn't love you. She was in love with the idea of you being a big star and making all that money. That's the only thing she loved. And when that didn't happen quick enough for her she bolted." He paused to stuff another chunk of tobacco into his mouth. "Gold digger, that's what that woman was. Nothing but a conniving gold digger."

"Yeah, I know. But what about those vows we took, huh? Doesn't that mean something?"

"Seems like it did to you," the bartender commented as he worked the tobacco between his cheek and gum. "Some people don't care about vows or keeping promises. The only thing they care about is themselves and their own needs."

Joby snorted and shrugged. "You've got that right. I was in the marriage for better or worse; she was just in it for better."

The idea hit him suddenly, like a sucker punch. He reached over the bar and pulled a pen from Houston's shirt pocket. Then, he retrieved a napkin from a pile next to a glass cup overflowing with green olives.

"What? What is it?" The bartender looked puzzled.

"Hang on a sec," Joby mumbled as he waved Houston off. He closed his eyes. A few moments later they flew open and he began scribbling furiously on the napkin. This is it, he thought, as he continued writing. Then, as if by divine inspiration, the melody descended upon him. Five minutes later he knew he had a hit on his hands. Ten minutes after that the next song came pouring out of a breached levee of creativity. Joby didn't stop writing until the bartender announced last call. He didn't leave the bar until a full hour after that when Houston finally had to kick him out and lock the doors.

36

Love Don't Pay the Bills

Sometimes, pain was good for you. That's what Joby thought as he strummed his guitar on the threadbare couch, naked except for a pair of worn boxer shorts with pictures of dancing beer cans dotting the fabric. After getting home from the bar he spent the rest of the night putting his words to music. By the time daylight peeked through the tattered blinds in his apartment he had rehearsed his new songs over and over, each time slightly tweaking the lyrics or melody. His favorite so far was "In It for Better," but "Memories of You" and "Paying My Dues" weren't far behind. He even had a working title for the CD: *The Dream*.

He was about to get up from the couch and make some coffee when the phone rang. Internally, he debated picking it up. After the third ring the part still tethered to his wife answered. Maybe Becky had come to her senses.

"I left a few things there," she snapped before he could say anything. "I'll stop by in an hour and pick them up."

"Becky, are you OK?" he asked with genuine concern in his voice.

She laughed. "I've never been better. I should have done this a long time ago."

"Hey, come on now, can't we talk about this?"

"Talk about what," she snarled. "The fact that you're a loser with no prospects and no future. Sure, we can talk about that. Want me to start?"

"Beck, look, it doesn't have to be this way. I love you."

An icy snicker shot through the line like a current of electricity. "You love me. Oh, wonderful! Hey, everyone, he loves me."

A gaggle of voices erupted in riotous hooting from the other end.

"Where are you?" he asked.

"None of your business. The only reason I called you was to tell you that I'll be stopping by to pick up the rest of my stuff and that I don't want to see you. Find somewhere else to go until I'm gone."

"I want to see you," Joby pleaded softly. "I want to talk about this…"

"Dammit, what don't you understand? I don't want to see you. I don't want to be with you. I want nothing to do with you. You've ruined my life. I should be living in Beverly Hills right now driving a Bentley and shopping on Rodeo Drive. That's what you promised, remember?"

He remembered. How could he forget? She'd reminded him of it every day during their marriage. Not subtle, playful reminders, either; angry, hurtful badgering that did nothing but cut him to the bone.

"I remember," he said softly, meekly.

"Yeah, so do I," she replied. "I wasted almost three years of my life on you. You said you were on the verge of making it big. Said the record deals would be coming in any day now. Liar."

"Beck, I didn't lie to you about anything. This isn't an easy industry to break into. I know I've got what it takes to make it. I just need that one big break. And it's going to happen."

"Save it. You've been saying that since the day I met you. When? When is it going to happen?" She answered her own question an instant later. "I'll tell you when: never. It's never going to happen for you. Want to know why? Because you're a no-talent loser, that's why."

"Becky, I love you..."

She cut him off before he could finish. "Love? Love don't pay the bills, sweetheart. Love doesn't get me my mansion and Bentley, *Joby*." She spat out his name like it was something distasteful. "You are still going by that name, aren't you? Joby Kidd. Jesus, even that made-up name of yours is stupid. No one's going to buy any song sung by someone named Joby Kidd."

She paused to take a breath. Before she could continue he spoke. "You're right, I guess I am a loser. I married you because I loved you, not because I wanted something from you or had any illusions that our life together was going to be perfect. I guess it's just taken me this long to realize what a cold, heartless woman you are. Come and get your stuff. I'll be gone so you don't have to worry about seeing me."

He was about to hang up but then stopped abruptly. "One more thing: someday, you're going to regret this. Mark my words. Someday, Joby Kidd will be a household name. You're going to hear my voice on the radio everywhere you go. And when you do, I want you to think long and hard about how you ended this. About how you treated me. Good-bye, Becky. Love may not pay the bills, but it should be enough by itself."

• • •

After hanging up inspiration struck again. "Love Don't Pay the Bills" came pouring out in a torrent of angry energy. When he was done writing he set his guitar aside, reclined on the couch and thought about this weekend's music showcase. He hoped at least one of the record guys showed up. He'd sent fifty e-mails out two weeks earlier and hadn't heard back from any of them. If this didn't work he was done with this whole country music fantasy. He'd told himself that many times before, but this time had a feeling that he really meant it. His last thoughts before sleep washed over him were of performing in front of an undulating sea of humanity in Texas Stadium. *Joby Kidd, Live in Concert.*

37

Welcome to the Broken Buzzard

At first Irvin Sampson wasn't sure he was in the right place. The mob packed tightly in the dimly lit bar looked appropriate: mainly white folks wearing ten-gallon hats, cowboy boots, oversized belt buckles, and Wrangler jeans. Most held a bottle of beer or some other cocktail. The only thing that looked out of place was the guy who had just walked out on stage dressed similarly. He was about to turn and ask the person next to him if he'd missed Joby Kidd. Before he could say anything the guy on stage answered his question.

"Hello, everybody, welcome to the Broken Buzzard. I'm Joby Kidd."

No way, Irvin Sampson thought. This was the last thing he'd been expecting to see tonight. Part of him wanted to leave, thinking this was some kind of joke, ala William Hung's fifteen minutes of fame following his *American Idol* appearance a few years back. He was about to knife his way through the crowd back to the exit when the guy on stage started strumming and singing. The lilting melody that came out stopped the would-be country music mogul in his tracks. Entranced, he eased back through the crowd, closer to the stage. The first few bars rolled gently, rising like ocean swells, building to an angry tidal wave of emotion until the last part of the chorus when everything slowed.

"How could I know her love would change, change just like the weather. I was in it for better or worse, she was just in it for better."

All around him the crowd erupted in gales of whistles and applause. From the stage, Joby Kidd smiled and tipped his hat graciously. He thanked the crowd and engaged in a bit of playful banter which segued easily into the next song. The transition was seamless, and Irvin was impressed. Not only was the guy a great singer, he also had a fantastic stage presence. That was something that couldn't be taught. You either had it or you didn't. Like Elvis or Mick Jagger or Garth Brooks.

"I'm going to continue with my new material," Joby said from the stage as he strummed his guitar. "This one's called 'Memories of You.'"

And he was off, milking each note and massaging the crowd like an old pro. A held note here, a wavering chord there, a perfectly timed whisper, like something shared between lovers. His performance was masterful, right up until the very end.

"I've got my memories of you, to keep me warm, to give me life, give me shelter from the storm. I don't know why our love had to die, but all I do is sit around and cry over you."

Irvin Sampson stared in awe. The music producer had a staunch history of heterosexuality, but right now he thought he was falling in love with Joby Kidd.

. . .

"That was amazing."

Joby turned and saw a tall black man dressed in jeans, boots, and a tan cowboy hat standing there. "Thanks," he muttered as he packed his guitar backstage. "I felt a little off tonight."

Irvin laughed. "If you call that off, then I'd love to see you when you're on." He reached into his coat pocket and pulled out his card. "I'm Irvin Sampson. You e-mailed me a couple of weeks ago. Sorry I never got back to you."

"Oh, Mr. Sampson." Joby reached out and examined the man's card. "I'm sorry, I sent out about fifty e-mails. Honestly, I don't even remember who all I sent them to."

Irvin laughed. "I understand, you don't have to apologize. And please, call me Irv."

They shook hands.

"You know," Joby started, "normally I'd be all nervous talking with a record company rep, but I'm just too wiped out from everything this week. All I want to do is get my stuff packed up and head home."

"Tell me about it," Irvin said, smiling. "Got time for a drink before you head out? I'd like to talk about your music."

Joby shrugged. He didn't really feel like hanging around the Broken Buzzard any more. This was probably going to be another dead end anyway. Wearily, he said yes to the drink in spite of himself.

In a secluded booth at the back of the bar Irvin spoke first. "You put on quite a show tonight. Impressed the hell out of me."

"Thanks," Joby said. "I've got to be honest with you though, Mr. Sampson…"

"Irv."

"Sorry," Joby smiled and nodded. "Irv. I've got to be honest with you. I've had it with this business. I know I've got the talent but getting noticed…shoot, that's darn near impossible. And I know this is going to sound cliché, kind of like one of my songs, but my wife just left me and I'm running out of money."

The singer's candor surprised him but he didn't let it show. "Sorry to hear about your wife," Irvin finally said. "I can empathize with you though. I'm just about done with this whole music thing myself."

It was Joby's turn to be surprised. "Really? Let me guess, your wife left you and your dog died. Or is it the other way around?"

Irvin laughed heartily. He leaned back, took his hat off, and wedged himself in the corner of the booth. "No, not quite that bad. You want the truth or should I make up some fancy-sounding bullshit?"

Joby laughed and nodded. "How about the truth. I'm tired of all the fancy-sounding bullshit in this business. It seems like everyone I've run into is full of it."

"Ha. Most of them are. I'm not though. What you see is what you get. And up until tonight I was planning on getting out of this business and heading off to Las Vegas to work security at a casino."

A quizzical look descended over Joby's face.

"Yeah," Irvin continued, "some country music mogul, huh? Give it all up and head out to Vegas to be a security guard. Just the kind of agent you want to hitch your wagon to, right?"

"At least you're being honest," Joby said with a snicker. "That's more than anyone else has been."

Irvin smiled. "Well, if you don't have that you don't have much. That's what my dad used to tell me."

Joby nodded slowly and folded his hand atop the table. "Since we're both being honest here can I tell you something without you getting offended? I mean, it's certainly not meant to be offensive."

"My friend," Irvin replied, "there is absolutely nothing in the world you could say that would offend me. I've been insulted by the best in my time."

Joby nodded. "OK, now don't take this the wrong way, but... you're not what I expected. I mean...well, you're black."

Irvin sat up in horror, examining his hands in disbelief and then touching his face. "What? No way! I don't believe it." Then he laughed.

"No, I'm not prejudiced or anything," Joby continued. "It's just that most people in this business are white. Like ninety-nine percent. Even the fans."

Irvin nodded and grinned broadly. "I know what you mean. Guess I'm just special that way. I've got a confession to make too.

You're not at all what I expected either. You're the first Asian country music singer I've ever run into."

"Guess I had that coming, huh?" Joby laughed. "Looks like we're both special. If nothing else, we'd make a unique team. The Asian and the Black guy. Since you're going to Vegas anyway we could hit the casino circuit. All those rednecks, shoot, they wouldn't know whether to shit or go blind."

The singer's folksy banter elicited another laugh from Irvin. "Mind if I ask where you're from? I mean, you've got no accent or anything."

"Sure," Joby replied. "Actually, I get that a lot. Most people who meet me for the first time either yell at me because they think I don't speak English, or ask me how I like it here in America. Shoot, I was raised here from the age of three months on."

"Adopted?"

Joby nodded. "The story goes like this: I was born in Seoul, South Korea and left on the front steps of a police station when I was a week old. They put me in an orphanage until I was adopted. From what my parents told me it was a real dump. I was malnourished and sick and had these open sores all over my body from bug bites. Anyway, my parents brought me back here and I was raised in Dallas. Lived in Texas my whole life."

"That's some story," Irvin said as he took it all in. "What about your name? Real or stage?"

Joby shifted in his seat and laughed. "Stage. My real name is Arthur Goldstein—my parents are Jewish. I didn't think 'Hopalong Goldstein' sounded too good for a country singer so I went with

Joby Kidd. Don't know why, really. I guess I just liked the sound of it."

"Man, you've really got all bases covered, culturally speaking," Irvin interjected. "Asian, Jewish. The only thing you're missing is black."

"Actually, I am part black." Joby laughed. "A few years ago I did some research and found my biological mother. Apparently, she was sixteen at the time and got pregnant by an American GI. He was black. You'd never know it by looking at me, though. I obviously got the looks genes from her."

"No offense," Irvin chuckled, "but you're a regular festival of nations. The Asian, Jewish, black country singer. I smell a biopic coming out of this. After we sell a few million CDs, of course."

"You sound pretty confident," Joby replied, a serious tone suddenly creeping into his voice.

"I am," Irvin said confidently. "Watching you tonight, man, you've got something special. Now all we need to do is get you into the studio and do some recording so the rest of the world can see how special you are. You ready to be a star?"

Joby shrugged. "Sure, why not."

38

Country-Voodoo Magic

One week. That was all it took to lay down and mix ten tracks in Cowboy Records' small but efficient studio in a dilapidated section of west Austin known for its drug houses. Joby brought in The Tumbleweeds, his backup band for the past two years, and together they worked what Irvin called "Country-Voodoo Magic."

From the mixing board behind a glass wall Irvin removed his headphones and gave the musicians a thumbs-up. "That sounded great," he said enthusiastically through a fog of static as he pressed the intercom button to the studio. "Come on back and take a listen."

Joby led the way, followed by bassist Pete Skillings, drummer LoJack Billups and his long-time friend and rhythm guitarist Alvin Summers. The musicians all took seats around the board next to Irvin.

"You really think it sounds good?" Joby asked. He wanted constructive criticism from Irvin, not just for him to say that everything sounded great.

Irvin folded his hands across his expansive chest and leaned back. "Yeah, I really do. You guys work great together. Everything is so seamless. Nice hooks and riffs. The rhythm and drums aren't overpowering."

Joby nodded. "Thanks. Sorry if I sound skeptical, but I've heard that before from other producers. They tell you everything sounds great, take your money, and run."

The members of The Tumbleweeds all nodded in agreement.

"I'm not like that," Irvin explained. "I know just saying that won't fully convince you, but in time, you'll see what I'm all about."

"So, what are you all about?" It was Pete Skillings who asked the pointed question, a note of derision in his voice.

Irvin was taken aback by the bassist's snide tone. "Well…like I told Joby, I'm all about honesty and finding classy country artists. That's it, straight up. No games no BS."

"Yeah, you may have told Joby all that stuff, but now I want to hear it," Skillings continued. "Joby doesn't bother sharing much with us lately." He turned and shot an icy glare at the singer.

"Come on, Pete," Alvin Summers interjected. "Just drop it, OK."

Skillings stood. "I'm not going to drop it, Al. And neither should you. When we started this band we all agreed that we were in it together. Then, you suggested we hook up with Joby. You said he was talented and could really bring something to the band. Well, last I checked, this band has become more about Joby and less about the rest of us. A lot less. Seems unfair to me."

"Pete, dude, come on, this isn't the time or place to talk about this…"

Skillings jumped in before LoJack Billups could finish. "Screw it, I'm tired of not talking about this. Before we go any further here we need to lay down some ground rules. It's supposed to be Joby Kidd and The Tumbleweeds, not just Joby Kidd." As an angry after-thought he added, "Goddammit."

Irvin stood and stepped from behind the board. "Look, I thought we went over all this already. From a marketing standpoint I think it's better if we simply go with *Joby Kidd*. That doesn't mean that any of you are less important in the band. But, Joby has written all the songs…"

"Fuck it," Skillings spat out disgustedly as he turned and faced the group. "You know what, do whatever you want. I'm done with all you assholes. I quit. And since I formed this band and came up with the name I'm taking that with me."

Skillings marched angrily back into the recording booth, slammed his bass into its velvet-lined case and stormed out of the studio. No one spoke immediately. After a few moments of uncomfortable silence Irvin chimed in, somewhat chagrined. "Does anyone know where we can find a good bass player?"

39

The Honeycomb

Outside, in the darkened alley behind the studio, Pete Skillings tossed the bass guitar into the trunk of his '78 Chevy Impala and slammed the hood shut. Enraged, he slid into the driver's seat and pounded his balled fists on the picked-apart foam ringing the steering wheel. This wasn't fair. He had started this band three years ago, not Joby Kidd.

For a moment he calmed, taking in a few deep breaths to clear the red from his vision. It worked. Thinking a bit more clearly he slid the key into the ignition and started the car. At the mouth of the alley he turned right onto a wide thoroughfare named after some kind of flower. As he accelerated through a green light at the next cross street he saw a clot of young men wearing saggy pants and dark T-shirts standing near an abused bus shelter on the corner. Knowing exactly what they were up to, he smiled. He could use a hit right about now, just to calm his frayed nerves. Crack always took the edge off, at least for a little while until the post-high crash sliced through your central nervous system like a buzz saw.

Cautiously, he sidled his car up alongside the group. Before stopping completely he swiveled his head in all directions looking for any sign of the police. Seeing none, he idled the car at the curb. One of the young men took notice and warily approached the open passenger side window.

"What you need, homey?"

"What you got?" Skillings nervously asked. He hated this part. Yes, he'd done it many times before, but you never really knew what was running through a drug dealer's head. Sometimes, they were as unpredictable as the weather.

The homeboy laughed and leaned into the open window. "Whatever you need, as long as you got the green."

Skillings nodded but didn't produce the cash. Years earlier, as a novice drug buyer, he'd done that once and gotten beaten and robbed. "I just need a couple rocks. If you've got them let's do this quick."

"Nothing on me, homes," the drug dealer shrugged. "Pull around the corner and we can dip into a honeycomb. Get you what you need and you be on your way."

Warning bells sounded in the back of his mind. He almost pulled away from the curb and sped off into the night. Normally, he wouldn't do this. It was already dangerous enough making drug deals out in the open, let alone going off to some honeycomb.

Instead of driving off, Skillings eyed the young man warily and nodded. "OK. But if there's any funny business I'm out of here."

The dope pusher laughed. "Won't be no funny business as long as you're cool. If not," he paused, a jagged grin spreading across his face, "me and some other homies might get real funny with you."

· · ·

The honeycomb was two blocks away, nestled between a dead-end alley and an abandoned warehouse sporting a toothless grin of broken windows. Until recently he'd never heard the term. He quickly figured out that a honeycomb was an abandoned house used by drug dealers and prostitutes to conduct their illicit business.

"I'll wait here," Skillings told the young man who sat in the passenger seat.

"Suit yourself, G. How much you want?"

The founder of The Tumbleweeds handed over five crisp twenties. "Get me an eight ball."

The drug dealer nodded, stepped out of the car and jogged around the side of the abandoned house and out of sight. He returned a few minutes later and retook the passenger seat.

"It's all good," he said as he handed over the plastic baggie containing 3.5 grams of crack cocaine.

Skillings held the bag up and examined the contents. Everything looked about right. "Thanks. You want a ride back to where I found you?"

"Damn, ain't you polite," the drug dealer said, smiling. "Sure, why not."

They rode in silence for a block before the dealer spoke. "You know, man, I was going to jack you up back there. Take your money and the rocks." He pulled his T-shirt up over his waist revealing the butt end of a small semiautomatic handgun silhouetted against dark washboard abs.

Skillings froze, his fingers tightening around the steering wheel. He thought about reaching for his own gun beneath the front seat but decided in a split second that wasn't the best idea. Any quick motion would probably spook the young dope slinger.

"But," the young man continued, "since you was nice enough to offer me a ride I decided not to do that. Tonight was your lucky night." He lowered the T-shirt and leaned back in the seat.

Gee, thanks for not robbing me. The thought ran through Pete's head but he decided against voicing it. Better to just nod and keep quiet. The sooner he dropped this young thug off the better. Then he could head home and puff his cares away in peace.

He was about to turn the corner when it happened. A supernova of multicolored lights flared behind him followed by the piercing wail of a siren.

"Goddamn, white boy," the drug dealer shouted as he glanced over his shoulder. "Fucking five-oh behind us."

A current of fear shot down Skillings' spine, constricting his testicles. Had he not made a conscious effort to hold his bladder he thought he would have pissed himself right there. This couldn't be happening. Not now, with sixty months hanging over his head from a previous narcotics conviction two years earlier. If they found the rocks in his car the judge was sure to send him to prison for every last one of those months. And not one of those cushy federal facilities where they sent white-collar crooks. No, he'd be going to a very different kind of prison. Some place like Angola or Marion, where sodomy was a way of life and a shank in the back a virtual certainty.

"Yeah, I know. Hang on." Skillings pressed the gas pedal to the floor. The Impala sputtered at first as gasoline flooded the carburetor. Then, with a low rumble it accelerated, shooting down the darkened street like a rocket.

"Shit...man, what the fuck you doing?" The drug dealer's tone betrayed his fear.

Skillings laughed nervously. "What do you think I'm doing? Trying to lose the cops. I can't let them catch me with this." He held up the baggie of crack.

"Then toss the shit out the window, dawg. I'm about to lose my gat." In a blur the dealer reached for his waistband, rolled down the window and tossed the gun out into the night.

Good idea, Skillings thought. Sure, he might still get busted for fleeing the police, but it sure beat getting caught with crack. Then he remembered the gun beneath him. How was he going to ditch that thing? He suddenly realized he was truly screwed. More screwed than he ever had been before in his life.

Before he could hatch a plan it happened. From out of the shadows a dog scurried in front of the Impala, crossing the street at a slow trot. Instinctively, Skillings swerved, cranking the wheel hard to the right and then back to the left. He missed the dog, barely, but hit a titanic oak tree on the boulevard head-on. As the car folded inward the drug dealer cannonballed through the windshield, impacting the oak headfirst, crushing his skull, killing him instantly. Skillings shot through the crumpled roof, his body squeezing through the shredded sheet metal like cheese through a grater. His last thought before losing consciousness was of his pregnant wife in Milwaukee. *I'm so sorry.* Then, everything went black.

Milwaukee

40

From Here to Maternity

Kara Skillings stirred beneath the sheets, roused by the jangling phone on the nightstand next to the bed. Sitting upright, she glanced around the shadow-cloaked room trying to clear the sleep cobwebs from her mind. After a few more rings she answered. The unfamiliar voice on the other end of the line was soft but resonated with stony authority.

"Mrs. Skillings?"

"Yes," she answered after clearing her voice.

A short pause from the other end followed by the sound of shuffling papers. "My name is Sergeant Heyer with the Austin Police Department. Is your husband Peter Martin Skillings?"

At the mention of Peter's name she suddenly became fully alert. "Well, technically, yes. We're separated. Why? What is it?"

A light cough came from the other end. This was the least favorite part of the police sergeant's job. He'd delivered dozens of similar notifications during his career, but it hadn't gotten any easier over the years. "I'm sorry to tell you this, ma'am, but Mr. Skillings was killed in a car accident about an hour ago."

Kara felt the blood drain from her face. A sudden feeling of vertigo washed over her, leaving her lightheaded. "Oh…what happened?" she mumbled softly, not sure if she'd said the words or merely thought them.

"I can't go into much detail," Sergeant Heyer informed her in an official tone. "All I can tell you right now, ma'am, is that Mr. Skillings was involved in an auto accident in which he was ejected from his vehicle. He was killed instantly."

She didn't know what to say. A hearty cheer seemed inappropriate, but she couldn't muster much in the way of sadness either. Indifferent was perhaps the best way to describe how she felt. After all, the dissolution of their marriage, and her subsequent return to Milwaukee, had been mostly his doing. His incessant lying and drug use had led her to issue an ultimatum two months earlier: get cleaned up for good or she was done. It looked to her like Peter had made his final decision. The drugs were more important than their marriage, or the impending arrival of their daughter in less than a month.

"Well…okay," she finally managed to say. "Thanks for calling."

"Are you going to be all right?" Sergeant Heyer asked, genuinely concerned.

The vertigo had abated leaving her with a clear head and a renewed sense of purpose. Finally, she could channel all her maternal energy into raising Haley. Peter's addiction had sapped so much of her strength over the years that she felt inadequate as a wife. Almost like she was caring for an adult child.

"Yes, thanks for your concern, Sergeant. I'm going to be fine. Honestly, this is almost a relief. I know that probably sounds insensitive, but Peter had a lot of issues. Drugs. That's the main reason we separated and I came back to Milwaukee. I always hoped he'd turn things around. Looks like he didn't though."

"I'm sorry to hear that," the sergeant replied. "I've seen drugs destroy a lot of lives during my career, most of them genuinely good people too. Sad."

"Thanks for the kind words," Kara said with a sigh.

"Anyway," Sergeant Heyer continued, "I hope everything works out for you. If you have any questions feel free to call me."

He rattled off his number which she hastily scribbled on an old Target receipt atop the nightstand. He said good-bye and the connection went dead.

• • •

In the kitchen she scooped six spoons of freshly ground coffee into a paper filter. Too wired to go back to sleep, she decided to simply start her day. She had to be up in an hour anyway to get ready for work.

The news from Texas hadn't come as much of a surprise. Deep down, she hoped that Peter would eventually get his act together and get completely clean, but she wasn't delusional. She knew that her hope couldn't make Peter get clean. Only he could do that.

To say that she hadn't loved him would be disingenuous. Early on, she did love him, very much, and he had been a good husband. Loving, caring, considerate. But then, he reverted to his old ways, first with the marijuana and then back to the coke. By the time she left Austin his drug use had spiraled out of control. He kept saying he was going to get help, but he never did. Her main concern was Haley. She didn't want her daughter around an unpredictable junkie. Now, the love she had once felt for him was gone. She didn't hate him—felt sorry for him, actually. To give everything up in your life that really mattered for a high—that was beyond sad. It was soul-piercingly tragic.

From the fridge she retrieved two eggs, a tub of margarine and half a loaf of wheat bread. The eggs she fried in a dab of olive oil while the bread toasted. Two minutes later she sat down at the small kitchen table and took a sip of hot coffee. After setting the mug down she blew lightly on the steaming eggs and dipped a corner of toast into the yellow yolk dome. The protective membrane broke, soaking the toast with delicious yolk as a lava flow of the yellow mucous dribbled onto the plate. Not the healthiest breakfast, she realized, but she didn't care. Not this morning.

She may not have loved her husband, but she certainly didn't want him dead. Not even for the large insurance policy he had hanging over his head. The only thing she'd really wanted was for him to change his life.

She was about to dip another triangle of toast when a dull pain, like a pinch, rippled through her abdomen. At first she barely noticed it, but after a few moments the sensation grew until she sat doubled up on the chair holding her stomach.

"Oh, God," she moaned, holding her bloated belly. The stark realization that something was seriously wrong dawned an instant later.

The pain stopped momentarily, but then returned with a vengeance, searing, unbearable. Kara felt something wet and warm between her legs. Fearing her water had broken she reached down. An instant later she recoiled in horror as she pulled her hand back, bloody and smelling of copper and yeast.

Panicked, she tried standing but fell in a crumpled heap to the floor. She could feel something moving inside her and the dread grew. Crawling across the blood streaked floor she managed to make it to the phone near the sink on the kitchen counter.

With great effort she held her belly with one hand and punched in 911 with the other. Before the connection could be made she stopped cold. A sudden explosion of pain raced through her brain followed by a pulsar of white light that flared brilliantly in her field of vision.

The phone fell to the linoleum floor just as Kara heard the voice on the other end say, "Milwaukee 911, what's your emergency?" The last thought that floated through her consciousness was of a meadow she had once played in as a child under clear blue skies. An instant after that, quicker than the blink of an eye, the meadow faded from her mind and she was gone.

• • •

"A brain aneurysm?" Grace Trainor's words came out slowly and seemed to hang in the air. "How? I mean…is that what killed Kara?"

Dr. Michael Sharp took a seat in the chair next to the woman and pulled the blue surgical mask from his face. "I'm afraid so," he said softly, empathetically. "It all happened very quickly, which isn't unusual in cases like this. The artery had probably been weakening for weeks, but the ultimate damage occurred in a matter of sec-onds." As an afterthought he added, "She didn't suffer. I know that's probably not much consolation."

Grace glanced sideways at the surgeon, her cheeks tear-stained and streaked with mascara. "That's good to know." A short pause while she fidgeted with a ring on her right hand, then, "What about the baby?"

Dr. Sharp glanced down at his hands and then back up at Grace. "We had to do an emergency C-section," he said gravely. "Believe it or not, the baby was delivered fine and is resting now. She appears to be perfectly normal and healthy. Amazing, really, after suffering that kind of trauma with her mother."

"Kara would have wanted it that way. Lose her life so her baby could live."

Grace dropped her head into her hands and let the tears flow. All of this had been so unexpected. Kara was young and had never shown any signs of being sick. But, as the surgeon next to her had said, an aneurysm was something that could go undetected for years. Then, one day, BANG, it could rupture and kill you almost instantly.

Grace suddenly felt a comforting hand on her shoulder and glanced to her left. Dr. Sharp looked deep into her eyes and smiled and nodded sympathetically.

"I'm so sorry for the loss of your sister," he whispered softly. "I can't even begin to imagine what you're going through right now. I mean, your sister...and the baby. So much sadness to deal with all at once."

Grace nodded and sat up straight, dabbing her eyes with a tissue the doctor held out to her. "Thanks. It is a lot to deal with. All of it. She was so young and looking forward to being a mother. Her husband…" Her words trailed off. She didn't think much of Pete Skillings—never had—and had told her sister that many times. Especially during his most recent relapse. The one that ultimately brought Kara back to Milwaukee.

"What about her husband?" the surgeon gently prodded.

Grace shook her head. "Nothing. It's just …well, he's a drug addict. A real lowlife. He's in a band and lives in Austin, Texas. Actually, they both did until a couple of months ago when Kara moved back here. She told me she'd given him an ultimatum to get sober or she was leaving. Needless to say, he didn't get sober."

"I get the impression she was a strong woman," Dr. Sharp said.

Grace nodded and allowed a nostalgic smile to creep in. "You have no idea. She was the type of person who stayed calm no matter what. The world could be collapsing around her and she wouldn't so much as raise her voice. Always calm. In fact, she saved my life when we were kids."

"Really? What happened?"

Grace glanced around the fourth-floor surgical waiting room. In the far corner a man napped fitfully on a small couch beneath a TV suspended from the ceiling. Fifteen feet to his left three children sat quietly around a small table coloring while two adults near them chatted in hushed whispers. On the other side of the room two young women scavenged for lunch in front of a wall of vending machines. One purchased a bottle of Coke and a bag of pretzels; the other settled for a Dr. Pepper and a King Size Snickers bar.

"I'll tell you," she finally said, "but I need to get some coffee and something to eat before this headache of mine gets any worse. Is there a cafeteria around here?"

The doctor nodded. "Yeah, downstairs. I'm starved too. If you can wait five minutes I'll join you. If you don't mind, that is?"

Grace shook her head. "Not at all. That would be nice. I could use the company, actually. Then, I can tell you all about the day my sister saved my life."

• • •

They waited in the hallway in front of the elevator doors. A gaunt man with sallow eyes wearing a white hospital gown shuffled past them pushing a stainless steel IV rack with a plastic tube snaking from the saline bag down to his arm. Grace thought the man looked like death warmed-over.

"How long have you been a surgeon?" she asked.

Michael cocked his head to the side and ticked off the time in his head. "Eight years," he finally said after completing the mental calculations. "I must be getting old. I had to think about that way too long."

Grace laughed softly while the doctor smiled.

"I suppose you're used to seeing people like that," she said, nodding her head in the direction of the shuffling man once he was out of earshot. "You're probably used to all sorts of tragedy."

Michael nodded slowly. "Yeah, I guess I am. It took awhile for me to be able to block all the misery out, but I'm a pro at it now. Maybe someday I'll go in for some much-needed therapy."

Grace laughed. "Therapy? You seem pretty normal. If anyone could use therapy it would be me. Especially after this morning."

The red number above the elevator finally stopped at their floor and the doors opened slowly an instant later. Before they could step inside a tall man stepped out. He wore black work boots, dark blue uniform pants and a tan short-sleeve oxford shirt with his name stitched into the fabric on the upper left side: *Chester*. His eyes darted nervously between Grace and the doctor and then down to the floor as he made his way down the antiseptic hallway and out the main doors at the far end.

In the quiet confines of the elevator after the doors had slid shut Grace spoke. "Strange guy."

Michael nodded. "Yeah, I've seen him around before. I think he works in the morgue. You're right though, he is a bit strange. I suppose you have to be to work down there."

"What about that look in his eyes? Freaky."

Michael shrugged and glanced at his watch. "I'm sure he's harmless. Probably into *Dungeons and Dragons* or something like that."

41

Crazy Chester

He tried to kiss her but her head was gone. In the heat of passion he forgot that he'd cut it off in the bathtub.

"Silly boy," Chester Dahl chided himself breathlessly as he thrust deeper inside the dead girl he'd picked up in the ghetto after leaving work. He called her Ethyl and she had been pretty. She'd told him she was eighteen and had just arrived in town from Madison. No family or any ties to Milwaukee. Just the clothes on her back and a few meager crumbs of meth in her pocket. She'd asked him if he wanted to party. *Sure, why not*, he'd said. The party hadn't lasted long. For her, at least. For him it was still a major rager.

He finished inside her vagina—as cold as deli roast beef—and pulled out. Depleted, he reclined on the couch and reached for her head which sat in a large steel kettle on the floor. "Thanks, honey, that was great," he said as he stroked her blood-matted hair. He gazed lovingly into her lifeless eyes and then pulled her head in close. His lips brushed hers, cold and blue, and a sexual shiver raced down his spine. He was ready to party again.

"Open up and say ahhhh," he muttered as he pried open her mouth and pushed his stiffening member past her frosty lips.

• • •

In the kitchen, ten minutes later, he tossed the kettle holding Ethyl's head into the fridge. He had to slide a jar of pickled testicles out of the way, as well as a plastic bucket containing a human heart. Before shutting the door he paused, mulling something over for a moment. He pulled out the bucket with the heart and set it on the counter next to the stove. He was hungry.

• • •

In bed, after consuming the entire heart with a side of potato salad, he flipped through TV channels, finally settling on the local news. The big story was about a missing person from Madison. The girl was the daughter of a Wisconsin state representative and had last been seen three days earlier. A photo of the girl popped up behind the anchor's right shoulder and Chester Dahl froze. It was Ethyl, only the anchor called her Mary Jane Marsden.

"Information obtained from the family indicates that Ms. Marsden may be in the Milwaukee area," the anchor explained. "Anyone with information concerning her whereabouts can call the Milwaukee Police Department's missing persons unit." The anchor's tone shifted from grave to bouncy and upbeat as he turned center stage over to the sports anchor, a buxom blonde Chester had fantasized about turning into a zombie sex slave and eating.

The whole zombie sex slave idea had come to him many years ago after he first realized that he could no longer control his impulses. The world, especially Milwaukee, was full of people who were expendable and wouldn't be missed.

As a kid he experimented with small animals—cats, hamsters, birds—cutting their heads open and fiddling around with their brains to see if he could turn them into zombies. Even though it never worked, he didn't give up. Small animals were one thing, but what if he could do it to a person? Turn someone into a lobotomized sex slave for his pleasure. No matter how hard he tried, though, he just couldn't get it right.

Now, ten years after his first attempt, he was no closer to a breakthrough than when he was a kid messing around with animals. Granted, it was still fun to screw, kill, and eat people, and not necessarily in that order either. He liked to change it up, just like he'd done with Ethyl tonight. Having sex with the living could be tiresome, and dangerous sometimes, if you happened to get a fighter. Sex with the dead was different, safer. The dead never complained that you were being too rough, or that it hurt or that they didn't want to take it up the ass. The dead just laid there and let you do whatever you wanted.

The blonde sports anchor finished her broadcast with a flirty smile and Chester flipped the TV off. Rolling onto his side, he threw an arm around Ethyl's stiffening body and pulled her close. He liked spooning, at least until they started rotting and stinking up his apartment. With the air-conditioning cranked he figured he had three more days to enjoy Ethyl's company, maybe even four. After that, he'd have to look for another companion. Good thing it was always hunting season in the neglected ghettos of North Milwaukee. And you didn't even need a permit.

In the semidarkness of his bedroom he rolled onto his back and gazed at the collage of photos plastered to the ceiling. He knew most normal people would find them gruesome—pictures of all his victims in various states of life, death, and dismemberment—but he didn't care. He knew he wasn't normal, had known it for a long time. All he really cared about was slaking his unquenchable thirst for sex and human flesh. The way he saw it, it wasn't entirely his fault. God had made him this way. If the Big Guy hadn't wanted him to go around killing and eating people He should have shut off the part of his brain that craved those things.

I want you. Ethyl purred like a kitten next to him.

Smiling, he rolled over and wedged his penis between her ice-cold buttocks.

"I want you too," Chester whispered into thin air as he gradually hardened and the world around him dissolved away.

•   •   •

Two more days was all she lasted. Even with the temperature in the apartment set at a very comfortable sixty degrees, the scent of decomposition had started to become evident. That was one of the funny things about dead bodies: they all decayed differently. Some you could hang onto for a week and a half, while others barely made it past a day or two. Part of it depended on the weather. The warmer and more humid it was, the quicker a corpse would rot. Still, some of it depended on the individual. Even dead, he reasoned, everyone was different.

Chester had learned long ago not to take any chances with odors, especially living in an apartment. Instead of chopping Ethyl up and freezing the cutlets, he decided to simply dump her in a vat of hydrochloric acid and let the rest of her melt away. Her head he decided to keep though; it fit nicely with six other skulls in the chest freezer he kept in the corner of the kitchenette. Those he wrapped in plastic. It helped keep freezer burn at bay.

With Ethyl liquefying, his thoughts turned eagerly toward the Hunt. Male or female tonight? Probably a female, but a male would do just fine. He went both ways so it really didn't matter much. He wasn't very picky. Man, woman, black, white, Asian. When you got right down to it, meat was meat. It all felt the same when you fucked it, and it all tasted the same when you ate it.

42

Dog Will Hunt

Chester didn't know why he did what he did. The reasons weren't really important. All he knew was that he had to do it. To him, killing and cannibalizing his victims was as fundamental as sleeping or breathing. That's not to say that he hadn't put a lot of thought into the reasons behind his behavior over the years. He was introspective, intuitive, and had wondered many times what drove him to do what society frowned upon. What it was, exactly, that made him tick the way he did. He felt no sense of remorse when he raped and killed someone, no guilt when he subsequently ate them.

Ultimately, he knew he wasn't normal. He may have been a cold-blooded killer with no conscience, but he wasn't delusional. As a child, when he'd get frightened at night thinking there was something hideous lurking in his closet or under the bed, his father used to reassure him that there was no such thing as monsters. It hadn't taken him long to realize that Dad was wrong. There were monsters, only they looked like average, everyday people most of the time. They looked like Chester Dahl.

· · ·

He spied her on the fringe of Clinton Rose Park near the corner of Fifth and Chambers. Beneath the halogen glow of the overhead streetlights she meandered slowly, glancing over her shoulder periodically at passing cars. A couple slowed, but then continued on, apparently not liking what she had to offer. Chester liked what he saw though. In the dancing shadows she kind of looked like Ethyl, except a bit older. Probably pushing thirty instead of twenty. He didn't care. Age was just a number.

He was about to pull over when he saw it approaching from the other lane. Like sharks cruising through chummed waters, police patrols roamed this area regularly, some in marked squad cars and others in unmarked vehicles. It was a notorious drug, gang, and prostitution hot spot. Here, johns got jacked up all the time by the lowlifes, thugs and whores who ran this neighborhood. The Beretta Cougar stuffed between the seat and center console made sure he was ready if that ever happened to him.

Instead of easing to the curb he continued driving, watching in the rearview mirror as the red taillights of the squad car continued southbound on Fifth Street and then turned off onto a side street a few blocks later. Actually, he was glad the police had been in the area. It reminded him to be vigilant, cautious. He didn't want to be one of these complacent guys who got caught because of something stupid. If anyone ever found out what he'd been doing all these years they'd send him to the gas chamber for sure. He wasn't quite ready to die, especially like some caged animal. When his time was up he planned on going out in a blaze of glory. Just not yet.

Half a block down he pulled onto a darkened service road that led into the park. Thirty feet in he stopped in front of a set of massive steel arms cemented to the ground and solidly chained shut. He killed the headlights and stepped out into the cool night air where the scent of the city greeted him. Raw sewage, car exhaust, and rotting garbage all mixed together to form a biting potpourri of urban decay. He didn't mind the odor, though. To him, rot smelled like sex.

Out of the shadows she finally emerged, her heels clip-clopping along the ribbon of cracked and broken sidewalk. She saw him and smiled. "You got a cigarette?"

He nodded and held out a crumpled pack of Camels.

"Thanks," she muttered as she fished one out.

Up close, beneath the harsh glow of the streetlight above, he realized the woman didn't look that much like Ethyl, after all. This one was prettier, less haggard looking, and had a confident, self-possessed air about her. A lot different from most of the streetwalkers he'd picked up and killed. Most of them were strung-out junkies afflicted with the wild-eyed look and involuntary muscle twitches of severe drug use. This woman looked almost normal.

"What's your name?" the woman asked as she took a puff off the cigarette.

"Donnie," he lied.

"Is that your real name, or a fake?"

"Does it matter?"

The woman smiled and shrugged. "Guess not. OK, then... Donnie, what are you doing out here? It's a bit too late to be out for a walk in this neighborhood."

Chester shrugged absently. "Couldn't sleep, so I thought I'd get out for a bit. Go for a drive. Do you like going for drives?"

"Depends."

"On what?"

Another puff from the cigarette, paired with a playful pout and slow teasing of hair. "The company."

"Oh, I'm very good company." Chester grinned. "You've never met anyone like me."

The woman smiled triumphantly and clapped her hands together. "Then it looks like I can go for a ride with you."

"My car's just around the corner," Chester informed her as he pointed down the sidewalk. "By the way, what's your name?"

The streetwalker slid her arm into his and pulled him down the sidewalk toward his waiting vehicle. "Does it matter?" she teased, and then laughed.

Not at all, Chester thought to himself as he smiled inside thinking of the fun that lay ahead of him. *Not at all*.

43

Turning the Tables

Hooooolllllddddstiiilllllllllllittttssgoingggggtttooobbeeeeokkaaayyy...

The victim stirred in the darkness hearing something garbled, blurred. The words—if that's what they were—sounded heavy and made no sense. Brief panic as the haze of sleep parted oh so slightly, like a shade being lifted on a window. Against a crushing weight, the victim tried sitting up. Had it worked? Don't know. Couldn't tell the difference bwetween lying down or sitting up. Couldn't tell, even, if they were alive or dead.

Pain, like a bomb blast, ripped through the victim's head, assuring them that they were still very much alive. Unless you could still feel things after death. They hoped not.

Eyelids felt like lead. So heavy, unable to open all the way. Throat, dry like sandpaper, hurt to swallow. Then, sound, less muddled this time, followed by a light slap on the cheek. More like a playful love tap.

"Time to wake up, sleepyhead."

The voice was familiar. The victim had heard it before, but where? Searing light from overhead suddenly filtered through slitted eyelids. The victim winced as though stabbed and turned away.

"Come on now, time to rise and shine."

The disembodied voice came again, still familiar, and more insistent now. This time, the ensuing slap across the face was harder and hurt like a bee sting. Flinching, the victim tried rolling into a protective ball but couldn't move; the body wouldn't do what the mind wanted.

"Where am I?" the victim croaked, startled by the inhuman echo of their own ragged voice.

"Does it matter?" the voice sing-songed mockingly. "Remember how you said that to me."

Fear, like nothing ever felt before, suddenly surged like a flash flood through a dry arroyo. The victim sputtered and coughed causing an orgasm of pain to shoot through what felt like every frayed nerve.

"Head...hurts. Everything hurts." Another desiccated croak, desperate and afraid.

From somewhere nearby shadows stirred, obscuring the overhead illumination. "It's for your own good," the stranger replied. "You'll feel better soon enough. Until then, I'm afraid it's going to hurt. Can't be helped."

"What..."

Before the victim could finish the stranger finished the question. "What are you doing here?"

The victim nodded mutely, smacking their parched lips together.

"Here, let me get you something for that," the stranger muttered.

Through the fog of pain shadows moved. From somewhere the sound of running water came, followed by muffled footfalls. Then, the victim's head was lifted and something pressed to their lips. Water. They drank greedily, sucking down every last drop before pleading for more.

"Not just yet," the stranger admonished. "You'll have to wait a bit. First we have some business to take care of."

Business? What was that supposed to mean?

A sudden tearing sound rippled through the air, followed by something cold being pressed to the victim's mouth.

"Wha..." The rest of the muffled words were swallowed by the sticky side of a strip of duct tape.

"I need to you be quiet, now," the stranger said in a voice that echoed with calm authority. "Because what happens next is going to hurt you more than it hurts me."

• • •

Chester woke sheathed in an icy film of sweat. Darkness pressed around him, cold and suffocating as he struggled to recall

where he was. Bits and pieces started coming back in brief snap-
shots as he forced himself to remember. A drive through the
ghetto; the smell of sewage and waste; Ethyl walking along a
sidewalk...

Wait, it couldn't have been Ethyl. Whatever was left of her was
either stuffed in his freezer or floated in a frothy sludge in a steel
drum back in his apartment. That sudden realization punched a
hole in the wall of confusion eliciting a stream of more memories
from last night: walking along the sidewalk with a strange woman;
getting into his car, which he had parked on the service road near
the park; pulling out into the night and suddenly feeling something
pinch his neck. At least it felt like a pinch. He remembered glancing
at the streetwalker and she was smiling. In one hand she held her
purse, while the other gripped a freshly depressed syringe containing a small amount of some kind of liquid.

Syringe?

A current of fear surged through him as more holes appeared
in the wall of mental chaos. On the other side, reality loomed,
stark and angry like a black thunderhead roiling on the horizon.
Something had gone terribly wrong, but what?

He closed his eyes and shook his head vigorously. Lightning
bolts of pain raced through his skull, but more of the fog lifted.
When he opened his eyes he realized he was shackled to a wall
in a basement, naked, except for his socks. Weak daylight filtered
through a small window above him; beneath him lay a filthy mattress. In the shadows the pad appeared stained with dark blotches.
Blood. His or someone else's, he wasn't sure.

He tried to speak but couldn't find his voice. The only thing that
came out was a tortured grunt, something like a wounded animal

might make. After a great deal of effort he managed to sit up on the mattress and prop his bare back against the cold concrete wall. More pain, dull and throbbing, this time from below his waist. With great effort he pushed his head forward and glanced down. What he didn't see made him suddenly scream.

44

Primum non Nocere

The killer woke before dawn and put her running shoes on. She grabbed a windbreaker from the gallery of neatly organized clothing and walked on down the hallway. Every day for her started with a five-mile run. No exceptions. She likened herself to the post office in that regard: *Neither rain nor sleet nor gloom of night shall keep me from my appointed rounds.*

The daily five-mile jaunt had been her routine for years, ever since her sophomore year in college when she weighed over two hundred pounds. Now, ten years after what she called her "whale phase," she was down to a svelte, toned one twenty. And she had no intention of ever going back.

In the kitchen she put down a banana and a quick cup of coffee. Another one of her routines. It provided just enough energy for her run. Anything more would have bogged her down and led to cramps; anything less and she'd make it no more than a couple of miles before her blood sugar level bottomed out. Neither scenario was good. She needed her daily run in order to function at her job. If she didn't run, then her work as a highly respected and skilled surgeon suffered, and she couldn't tolerate that. Neither could her patients.

As she finished the last swig of black coffee her thoughts drifted back to last night's activities. The Hunt had been a success. The man in the basement—Donnie, or whatever his real name was—still sat chained to the wall, bound and gagged. He'd stopped struggling shortly after losing consciousness after she'd separated his testicles and penis from the rest of his body. Before the operation she'd given him a shot of morphine, but not too much. She wanted him to feel some of the pain so she administered just enough to take the edge off, but not enough to completely knock him out. That would have been no fun at all. It was better when they felt the icy scalpel slide under the wrinkled edges of their scrotum. The look of sheer terror and desperation in their eyes, that was priceless. She thought about that Master Card commercial and laughed: *Roll of duct tape, $5; Razor-sharp scalpel, $30; Savoring the look of horror in your victims' eyes as you slice off their manhood, priceless.*

She wasn't sure how many men had come before Donnie. She'd stopped counting after the first ten, and that had been a couple years ago. Still, even after all these years, the Hunt had not gotten old. In fact, it was one of the few things that she truly looked forward to. Everything else, even work sometimes, had its dull moments. The Hunt, however, was never dull.

The Hunt. That's what she'd called it all these years. She saw it as her way of giving back to the world, albeit in a fashion a bit less orthodox than people like Mother Teresa or Gandhi. Her goal wasn't to save souls; that she left to God, if he or she existed. Her aim was more pragmatic and simple in an earthly sense: rid the streets of as many johns as possible.

They were loathsome creatures, johns, trawling the back alleys and side streets of the ghetto looking for any young woman strung out enough to suck them off for twenty dollars, or do a half and half for thirty. Then, there were the sickos out there who thought it was fun to carve these poor girls up and dump them on the side of the road or in some trash bin. The prevailing wisdom, even among most cops, was that no one would miss these girls anyway; they were just whores, sluts—pieces of meat to be used and discarded like trash. She didn't think like that. Not at all.

Once, long ago, she had been treated like a piece of meat and left to die. That had been in another lifetime, though, before she knew where her ultimate destiny lay, and well before taking her oath to "*first do no harm*" after graduating from medical school. The way she saw it, she wasn't really harming anyone other than people who had it coming anyway. Society benefited, as did those poor girls walking the streets selling their bodies. She knew she couldn't help all of them; she was only one woman, after all. But she certainly could do her part. A few dead johns was better than no dead johns, wasn't it?

At the sink she rinsed the coffee mug and set it on the top rack of the dishwasher. She was about to shut the stainless steel door but stopped. Reaching inside, she shifted another coffee cup so that the ceramic handle lined up perfectly with the latest addition. Then she smiled and closed the dishwasher door. She knew if she didn't fix the cup the misalignment would have nagged at her all day. Even with dirty dishes she was organized. She wondered if that made her crazy. This time, her smile broke into full-blown laughter. The OCD didn't necessarily make her crazy, but killing people she picked up on the street probably did. *That's OK*, she thought to herself, still smiling. *I can live with that kind of crazy.*

45

The Great Emancipator

Half alive or half dead, he couldn't tell. Every move he made on the bloody mattress brought more searing pain, each breath, the sad realization that his life was slowly ebbing away.

Chester willed his eyes to open. How long had he been out? Minutes? Hours? Days? He didn't know. All he knew at this moment was that it was dark again. Faint shafts of moonlight, pale and anemic, filtered through the glass-block window above his head. In the suffocating darkness he shifted by accident. Sheets of pain raced from his damaged groin and he yelped again.

"How are you feeling, sweetheart?" The disembodied voice in the darkness caused him to jump. More pain followed, sharp and hot like a branding iron.

"Who...who's there?" he stammered on the verge of tumbling back into shock.

"Just little ol' me," the woman chirped happily from behind a veil of shadows on the other side of the room.

It sounded like she was glad to be here with him. "Don't hurt me anymore," he pleaded in a voice that was soft and weak.

Soft, melodic laughter. "I'm not trying to hurt you," she explained. "My goal is to liberate you. Men like you, you walk around like slaves. Slaves to your cocks. Now, you don't have to be a slave anymore. You can be the master of your own destiny. You've been emancipated. Consider me your Abraham Lincoln."

"Why..."

She cut him off again. "Why am I doing this?"

Chester nodded and then realized she probably couldn't see him through the darkness. "Yes, why?"

From the other side of the room a bright light sliced through the gloom, blinding him. A loud thud followed accompanied by the sound of shuffling. Instinctively, he tried shielding his eyes but his arms remained locked in place, still chained to the wall. A few moments later his tormentor stood by his side, flashlight in one hand folding chair in the other.

"Do you really want to know why I'm doing this?" the woman asked as she took a seat across from him in the folding chair. She focused the intense beam of light on his face and he squinched his eyes shut.

"Yes...please...can you turn the light off?"

She laughed. "No, sorry, can't do that. Now open your eyes and look at me."

"Too bright…I can't open them…"

The woman shook her head, sighed dejectedly, and stood. She retreated to a work bench on the other side of the room. In the shadows he could see her fiddling with something. The sound of shifting tools and steel sent a shiver down his spine. *What's she doing?*

An instant later the basement was filled with blaring music.

"Ooops, too loud," she said apologetically as she fidgeted with the radio. The music volume receded to a more moderate level. "Do you like country music?"

From the mattress he nodded slowly as she glanced over her shoulder at him. Fear coursed through him causing his heart to pound like a bass drum. Any second now he expected it to burst through his chest, just like the creature in the movie *Alien* had done. For the first time ever he could finally empathize with his victims. He had to admit that he didn't like it one bit.

"That's good," she continued. "I like to have it on in the background most of the time." She stopped and cocked her head toward the radio as the DJ cued up the next song, a new release that had quickly climbed the charts to number one. "Oh, I love this song. It's by this new guy from Texas."

A couple minutes of soft guitar and gentle background melody ensued, followed by a plaintive chorus: *"…I was in it for better or worse, she was just in it for better."*

All through the song Chester watched the woman move and sway to the swells and troughs of the lolling rhythm. It appeared as though she was in a trance, mesmerized by the music emanating from the small radio. Then, the song faded away and so did her reverie. She marched back to his location with something in her right hand.

"Are you going to keep your eyes open now?" she asked as she refocused the light on his face.

"Look, I'm s-s-sorry, I can't with that light..."

She didn't let him finish. In one swift motion she reached out, pressed his head to the mattress, folded his eyelids back and stapled them to the base of his brow. His howls echoed through the basement as she plastered another strip of duct tape over his mouth. She stepped back, obviously pleased with the results, and retook her seat.

"Maintaining proper eye contact is very important to me," she explained evenly. "Now that we've established that, I can finally tell you why I'm doing this. Of course," she paused, redirecting the light away from his face and focusing the beam on the wall above his head, "it's going to be the last thing you ever hear."

46

The Last Days of May

They took turns fucking her in the back of the Dodge minivan.

Davey Stewart went first, never even bothering to put a condom on. He simply placed one hand over the girl's mouth while his brother Fred and their drug dealer friend Pat Horgan held her down and spread her legs far apart. Davey managed to squeeze inside the girl after a few forceful pushes, and with a bit of assistance from a palmful of frothy spit.

Fred went next, plowing the young girl while she screamed and kicked, desperately trying to free herself from beneath him. After pulling out and finishing on her stomach, Fred slapped her hard across the face. Once, twice, three times, each smack more forceful than the last. Then, he wrapped his hands around her throat, crimping the blood flow to her brain for a few seconds until she finally passed out.

"Why'd you have to go and do that?" Pat Horgan slurred angrily, the scent of whiskey strong on his breath. "You knocked the bitch out."

"So what," Fred muttered absently as he struggled to catch his breath. "You can still fuck her."

Horgan glanced down at the girl, smiled and shrugged. "Yeah, I guess I can." He loosened his belt and let his trousers fall in a bunch around his ankles. A few seconds later he was deep inside the unconscious girl, pumping furiously as though his life depended on it. After accommodating the Stewart brothers she was wet and loose. Pat Horgan didn't care though; sloppy seconds were better than nothing. Especially this way. He had no idea gang rape could be so arousing.

"Take it...yeah, you fucking bitch. Take it..." Horgan emptied himself inside the girl and collapsed on top of her just as she started to regain consciousness.

"She's coming to," Fred said anxiously as he released his hold on the girl's right leg.

"What should we do?" Pat Horgan asked as he hitched up his pants, an edge of nervous energy in his voice.

"Gimme those," Davey said, pointing to a dirty red and white bandana and brown extension cord stuffed under the front passenger seat amid a pile of empty beer cans and discarded fast-food wrappers.

Fred snatched the items from beneath the seat and handed them to his brother. Before the girl could come to, Davey wrapped the oily cloth around her eyes and knotted it tightly behind her head. Without hesitation he took the brown extension cord, rolled the half-naked, cum-stained girl onto her stomach, and tied her hands snugly together behind her back. Finished, he raised his arms triumphantly and laughed gruffly. "Did you guys see that expert hogtie? World record time."

A round of drunken laughter circumnavigated the group, dampening the nervous energy circulating through the van.

"Dude, you should be on the rodeo circuit," Pat mumbled almost unintelligibly.

"Yeah," Fred nodded in agreement. "The *Fuck-and-Rope-Dumb-Bitches* rodeo circuit. We could just pick up little runaways like this and keep them in a stable where we can have our way with them. Then, once we're done, we let them run free while we calf-rope 'em."

More laughter erupted from the group, drunken, hysterical.

From the grimy floor of the van the girl stirred, straining weakly against the ligature that bit into her wrists. Half-conscious, she mumbled something and tried rolling onto her back. After a few moments she gave up and turned her head to the side. That's when she started screaming again.

"Goddammit, shut up!" Davey yelled at her.

But she didn't. Instead, her terrified shrieking increased to ear-piercing levels. Furious, the Stewart brothers rolled her over while Pat Horgan grabbed the girl's panties from near the wheel well, rolled the cottony fabric into a ball and stuffed them into her mouth. She gagged on her own sweat and vaginal juices, her body spasming wildly as she fought to gulp in precious oxygen.

"That should keep her quiet," Fred mumbled as he ran a hand across his sweat-dimpled brow. "Now what?"

Davey, the de facto leader of the group, thought for a moment. Not many options at this point, the sober part of his brain told him. Kick her loose and she'd run to the cops and ID them in a heartbeat. Sure, she'd probably tell them that she'd keep quiet; keep what happened here to herself. Who wouldn't say that? That would be risky for them, though. The way he saw it right now, there was only one option.

"Get her out of the van," he instructed his brother and Pat Horgan.

Both young men shrugged and nodded. They seemed to know what was coming.

Outside, in the harsh glow of the van's headlights, they dropped her on her back on the dusty desert floor. She landed with a blunt thud and grunted as the wind was forced out of her lungs in one large gasp.

Pat Horgan and the younger Stewart brother pulled her up and forced her onto her knees. Like a malevolent jury, all three men stood before her while Davey pulled her head up by the hair. Through blurry eyes she gazed at her tormentors, her face bruised and battered, tear-streaked and bloody. Instead of seeing fear in her eyes, though, Davey saw something else—a look of pure, undiluted hatred that caused a chill to zip down his back and his testicles to shrivel. Unnerved, he let her head drop back toward the ground.

"So long, bitch," he muttered uneasily as he pulled a box cutter from his pocket and pressed the razor-edge to her neck.

47

Two Roads Diverged

May Jung felt the cold steel press up against the tender underside of her throat. She closed her eyes, bracing herself for what she knew was coming, and started muttering a soft prayer under her breath. After a moment she stopped. If God hadn't heard her pleas to this point why would He intervene now? Maybe it had been His plan all along to have her die like this—raped by these animals and beaten to a bloody pulp.

If only she hadn't decided to walk home after finishing her shift at the library. Her boss had offered to give her a ride, but she'd declined. Home was less than a mile away, she'd told him, and it was a perfect night for a walk.

"Just be careful," Ted Denby admonished her as he unlocked his car and slid behind the wheel. "There are a lot of creeps out there."

"Don't worry, Ted," she said and laughed dismissively. "Ridgecrest isn't exactly a hotbed of crime. Although, now that I think about it, Mrs. Jenkins' cat did get stuck in a cactus last week."

In spite of himself, he laughed. "You're way too trusting, young lady. When I lived in New York..."

She cut him off before he could continue. "I know, I know. Murders and rapes every day. Drug dealers. Son of Sam. But, Ted," she paused as she slung her backpack over her shoulder and tucked an errant strand of dark hair behind her ear, "this isn't New York."

"That's true," he replied as he started his car and rolled down the window. "But there are bad people everywhere. Even in peaceful Ridgecrest, California."

"I'll keep that in mind," she said, beaming sweetly. "See you tomorrow."

A quick smile and wave good-bye and the head librarian was gone.

If only...

The words echoed through her mind. None of that mattered now. She could second-guess her decision to walk home from now until the end of eternity and it wouldn't make a bit of difference. The reality of things was that she was here, kneeling in the dirt beneath a pale moon and spectacular canopy of stars, about to die at the age of fifteen.

Then, without warning, it happened. Like a brittle twig, something in the deep recesses of her mind seemed to snap. It didn't hurt; actually, it felt good. Liberating. Years later she would realize that it was at that moment that a road had diverged in her mind, forking in two very opposite directions, just like in Robert Frost's poem. In that instant, like a newborn baby, June entered the world, ready to protect her psychologically conjoined twin. Ready to do the things that May wasn't equipped to do.

Everything's going to be all right, June softly reassured her other half. *Let me handle this.*

Had she not been terrified beyond comprehension, May might have jumped at the voice that echoed in the dark channels of her mind. Instead, she simply looked up at the young man who held the blade to her throat and let June take over. And as she did, May felt the blade pull jerkily across her throat. The last thing she remembered before losing consciousness was hearing June's reassuring voice.

Stay with me, babe. We're going to make it out of this. And when we do, things are going to be different. A lot different.

48

Omega

In the gloom of the basement June leaned forward and tugged at the collar of her turtleneck. "This is my constant reminder of that night," she said to Chester as she traced the pink line of scar tissue that crisscrossed the base of her throat. "They left me for dead, but I made it."

She paused and quickly corrected herself. "*We* made it, actually; me *and* May. The police found us two days later in the desert just outside Ridgecrest. Another few hours and they said we'd have been dead. Ever since then we've taken care of each other. I'm the strong, silent one and she's the smart, ambitious one. We make a killer team."

June laughed. "Sorry, no pun intended." She fidgeted with a chipped nail for a moment, finally gnawing off the ragged edge with her teeth. "Anyway, some story, huh?"

Silence greeted her. Reaching down, she grabbed the flashlight and redirected the beam toward the mattress. Propped against the wall like a limp ragdoll sat Chester, head cocked to one side, tongue lolling obscenely with a dangling thread of pink drool hanging down. He stared back at her through lifeless eyes ringed with dark circles of crusted blood. She thought he looked like a rabid raccoon; or Heath Ledger as The Joker in the most recent *Batman* movie. Funny.

"Looks like I bored you to death with that story." June shrugged. "I guess you can't please everyone."

In the darkness she stood from the chair and stretched. She flipped the flashlight off and switched on the fluorescent lights embedded in the ceiling overhead. Now came the real work: disposing of the body. Truth be told, it wasn't really that hard. She had forty acres to work with, and no close neighbors to go around poking their noses where they didn't belong. Still, this part wasn't as much fun as the Hunt. It was necessary, though, and it had to be done properly. She had no intention of getting caught. Ever.

At the workbench on the other side of the basement she turned off the radio and packed away the industrial-size staple gun. As she set to work slicing up Donnie—or whatever his real name was—happy thoughts danced through her head, as well as the sweet melody of her new favorite song:

I was in it for better or worse, she was just in it for better...

49

He Seemed Like a Nice Guy

Police find 'house of horrors' in north-side apartment; renter's whereabouts unknown

By Jack Doff of the Journal Sentinel

MILWAUKEE—Milwaukee police made a gruesome discovery yesterday after being called to a north-side apartment complex. Residents of the *LaBlanche Villas* called 911 complaining of a foul odor coming from an apartment forthe past few days. After gaining entry into the apartment, officers found drums containing human body parts being dissolved in acid. Authorities also reported discovering four severed heads in a freezer as well as various body parts in the refrigerator.

"At this time we're still trying to figure out what went on in thisapartment," Detective Sergeant JC Caldwell said. "We have an extensive crime scene here. It's a house of horrors. Honestly, I've never seen anything like this."

According to police, the whereabouts of the tenant in apartment 235 are unknown. Police declined to identify the resident, but said that a lone male is listed on the lease documents and that he is considered a suspect.

"Right now, we have seven different bodies we're in the process of identifying," Caldwell said. "In addition to murder, we're also looking into the possibility that there was torture, cannibalism, and necrophilia going on inside this apartment."

According to other tenants, the resident of apartment 235, identified only as Chester, has not been seen around the building for at least two weeks. Unusual, they say, for a man who spent much of the time in his apartment.

"I didn't know him real well," said longtime *LaBlanche* resident Jerry Jefferson. "He mostly kept to himself, but he seemed like a nice guy. Evenhelped me dress a deer I bagged last fall. He was real quiet, except for the times it sounded like he had power tools going in his apartment."

San Francisco

50

City by the Bay

Before leaving for San Francisco International, Gary B. Williams kissed his sleeping wife lightly on the forehead and brushed aside a stray lock of her blonde hair. He turned, grabbed his suitcase from next to the nightstand and headed quietly for the door.

"Is that all I get?" a soft voice purred sleepily before he could shut the bedroom door behind him.

In the darkness he stopped and smiled. He should have known better; Allison never let him leave that easily, no matter how early it was.

"I didn't want to wake you," he replied as he padded back across the room.

She patted the mattress and moved back, making room on the edge of the bed for him. Gary set the suitcase aside and took a seat atop the crisp bed sheets.

"It's way early," she mumbled, playfully tugging on his tie, her voice still heavy with sleep. "You've got a few minutes more before you really have to leave, don't you?"

"As a matter of fact, I do. Why? What do you have in mind?" He chuckled softly, feigning innocence.

She tugged hard on his tie, pulling him toward her. Their lips met urgently in an explosion of carnal energy. Despite her morning breath he kissed her deeply, hungrily pushing his tongue past her lips.

"Let me show you what I have in mind," she whispered breathlessly into his ear as they helped each other out of their clothing.

•　•　•

Stupid. Because of his easily persuaded libido he was now running late.

After Allison finished riding him, Gary nestled his head snugly into the plush comfort of his pillow and closed his eyes. Just for a few moments, he'd told himself. Just to catch his breath.

Unfortunately for him, sleep crept in on silent paws and pulled him under. A few moments of relaxation had turned into an hour of bottomless slumber; the kind of sleep that only heady lovemaking could induce. The only thing that saved him was a swift kick to his side from Allie. Another one of her nightmares, or so she said. Over the years he'd gotten used to the nocturnal assaults. She maintained they were accidental and that she could never remember them, but he told her he had his doubts about that. That usually elicited a laugh and a sly wink from her.

"Even asleep you're not safe from me," she would chide him and then follow up with a playfully menacing mad scientist laugh: *Mwaaah aaahh aaahh aaahh aah!*

Despite running late, Gary found it hard to be terribly angry. As usual, the sex had been amazing. Plus, he hated these weeklong business trips to Chicago as much as she did. Most of the guys in his office couldn't wait to get away from their spouses, but not him. He actually liked his wife, and didn't care to spend one minute longer away from her than he had to.

"Just wait," Bill Dobbins, a senior account executive in acquisitions had cautioned him last week. "You've been married for what, three years? Give it a little more time before she turns into a nagging witch. That's when you'll start to hate her. It's inevitable. Happens to even the best of us."

As he coached the black Mercedes CLK550 along Highway 280 Gary wondered if the senior account executive was right. After the years started piling up in the rearview mirror of their marriage would he and Allie end up hating each other like so many other couples they knew? He hoped not. Still, the way the world worked these days, you never knew. He didn't plan on doing anything to mess up their marriage, and he didn't think Allie would either. He was smart enough, however, to know that fate had its own way of intervening sometimes. If there was even such a thing as fate. He wasn't sure about that, either.

He was about to flip channels on the satellite radio when the next news item stopped him: serial murders in Milwaukee. He'd heard something about it yesterday, but caught only the tail end of the story. After listening intently to the end of the story a shiver of revulsion raced through him.

"What is wrong with people?" he muttered under his breath. Cannibalism. Necrophilia. Heads in a freezer. Someone must have done a number on that poor soul when he was a kid. The fact that it happened in Wisconsin didn't surprise him; lots of nuts seemed to come out of there. He wondered what it was about America's Dairyland that drove people stark-raving mad. Was it the long, cold winters? Or maybe there was something sinister in the beer and cheese.

Gary reached for his coffee and took a sip. He set the stainless steel thermos back in the cup holder and trained his gaze on the freeway ahead of him. What he saw made his blood run cold: a river of red and white brake lights snaking through the early morning pitch as far as the eye could see.

Great.

Furtively, he checked the rearview mirror and quickly glanced over his shoulder. If he timed things just right he might be able to get far enough over and snare the next exit. If not, so much for making it to Chicago today. And so much for landing the new Axiom Express account.

Seeing no oncoming traffic he signaled and quickly cut across two lanes. The exit was coming up on him fast so he tapped the brakes. At the last second he swerved, shooting up the exit ramp and around the wall of stopped cars in front of him. Elated, he breathed a sigh of relief. He might just make the flight after all.

• • •

In the kitchen, an hour after her husband had left for the airport, Allison Williams set about on her morning routine. Fresh pot of strong coffee; two pieces of wheat toast topped with a blanket of creamy peanut butter and banana slices; glass of extra pulp orange juice and her laptop.

Normally, when Gary was home, they'd have breakfast together and then head opposite directions for work. She traveled west toward her law office; Gary went southeast into the heart of the city. Weeks like this, though, when he was out of town, her pace slowed a bit. Morning run, followed by a hot shower, breakfast, and perusing the news online.

Frankly, she liked it this way more and more. After three years the man she had pledged to remain faithful to in sickness and in health was starting to get on her nerves.

Not big things, really; mainly just a lot of small things. Death by a thousand cuts was how she saw it.

Leaving the toothpaste tube uncapped. Dirty socks scattered across the bedroom floor. Snoring, loud and labored like a growling bear. Peeing in the shower. That one Gary claimed not to do, but she knew better. *All* men peed in the shower.

Then, there was the sex. It was good, but not like it used to be. Things had changed. Gone were the anticipation and excitement of their early years together. Now, most of the time, things in that department were monotonous, robotic. This morning had been good, but that was because she'd been half asleep and thinking of someone else. Someone who was a friend, but had suddenly become so much more.

· · ·

"He's gone." Allison's voice resonated with excitement as she spoke into the mouthpiece. Breakfast was done and she had just gotten out of the shower.

"It's about time," the voice on the other end of the line said almost breathlessly. "I can't wait to see you."

Allison giggled like a teenager with her first crush. "Me too. Get here quickly, OK?"

"Be there in fifteen minutes."

A gentle computerized beep and the connection ended.

51

A Pleasant Surprise

Gary ran through the terminal just like OJ Simpson had done in those commercials—leaping luggage and dodging old ladies. That was before the football hero became a murderer. He remembered those ads vividly. He'd been a kid at the time, and the Juice had been one of his favorite football players. Truth be told, he was still somewhat fond of him. Not because OJ was a stellar citizen, but because he'd managed to sell a fistful of the Hall of Famer's mint-condition rookie trading cards for almost ten grand after the infamous televised car chase through Los Angeles in 1994. It was funny how the world worked sometimes; one person's calamity could be another's windfall.

Passing a bank of television screens showing arrival and departure times, he slowed, craning his neck to catch a glimpse of his flight number. Seeing nothing, he hitched his carry-on bag over his shoulder and picked up the pace, his black loafers click-clacking loudly off the tiled floor of the terminal.

After leaving another fifty yards of terminal in his wake he skidded to a stop and watched desperately as his flight backed irretrievably away from the Jetway and onto the tarmac. Dejected, Gary cursed softly under his breath and hung his head as he turned back toward the way he had just come. At least he didn't have to run through the airport like OJ Simpson anymore.

• • •

"Hey, honey, I missed my flight and wasn't able to get another one until later this afternoon. I'm on my way home. See you in a bit if you're there."

Gary disconnected the call and casually flipped the cell phone onto the leather seat next to him. Ahead of him, past the majestic spires of the Golden Gate Bridge, the sun blazed a brilliant burnt orange as it hung over the far horizon. On the radio they were still talking about the serial murders in Milwaukee. The morning host had a forensic psychologist on the air trying to explain the behavior of serial killers. She used terms like antisocial personality disorder, McDonald triad and personality disintegration in describing him, and went on to say that violence like this is all about power and complete domination.

Gary listened intently, fascinated by what he was hearing. In college he'd taken a sociology class to fulfill some obscure liberal arts requirement and actually enjoyed it. He found the section on serial killers the most fascinating and even thought of changing his major to criminology and maybe pursuing a career with the FBI. Back then, he thought he'd look good in a trench coat and sporting a badge and gun. Sometimes, he would even rehearse his introductions in front of a mirror in the most authoritative voice he could muster: "Special Agent Gary Williams, FBI."

Looking back, he was glad he hadn't chosen that route. He didn't know how much FBI agents made now, but he was certain it was nowhere near the seven hundred fifty thousand he was scheduled to pull in this year. Plus, he didn't think he could handle some of those crime scenes or investigations. Too depressing. The most stressful thing he had to worry about in his current line of work was making his quota, and for someone with his outgoing personality that had never been a problem.

Still, there had been regrets along the way. Missed opportunities he wished he could revisit and somehow alter. Like Tara Van Dyke, his girlfriend during his last two years of college. At the time he thought she was going to be the one he'd spend the rest of his life with. That was before she ended their relationship after telling him she'd found someone else with whom she was more compatible. He knew the truth though. He'd basically pushed her away with his unwillingness to commit to anything past the next week. He wanted to share the rest of his life with her, but seemed unable to think that far ahead. In his opinion, that's what forced her away.

In spite of everything, their breakup had been relatively amicable. They had even managed to remain friends through the years and still kept in contact. Allison even knew Tara and liked her. For that he was glad. He hated to lose a close friend over petty jealousy. Fortunately, his wife wasn't the jealous type. She trusted him, and he trusted her. As far as he was concerned he had the perfect wife and perfect marriage.

It wasn't that he wanted to pursue something with Tara. He loved Allison more than anything. For him, it was more about the "what ifs." What if he'd married Tara instead of Allie? How would that have changed his life? He supposed he could "what if" from now until the end of time and never really know how things may have turned out differently. Holding on to the past too tightly could drive you crazy, he thought.

• • •

Instead of slipping into the garage he parked the Mercedes on Bentley Street outside the house. He didn't plan on being inside long. If Allie was home he'd see if she wanted to hit the gym with him for a quick workout and then maybe an early lunch at Benny's. When he was out of town he knew she didn't head into the office until later in the morning. He never asked her why; it had just been that way for the past couple of years.

Inside, he tossed his keys on the granite countertop in the kitchen and stepped out of his shoes.

"Allie, are you here?" he called as he stepped into the family room.

No response, but he thought he heard a noise coming from upstairs. Probably getting ready for work, he thought, as he made his way to the staircase. More noise, like moaning, muffled and faint. An alarm went off in the back of his mind. Maybe she was hurt.

Gary mounted the steps and quickly made his way to the top. The moaning was louder now and unmistakably sexual in nature. A sly smile crept across his face. Such a little nympho. It had to be the Pink Dolphin, her vibrator. Apparently, in his haste to make it to the airport, he hadn't fully satisfied her before leaving this morning. *I'll take care of that*, he thought happily, as he unbuckled his pants and made his way eagerly down the hallway to the bedroom door that sat wedged open halfway.

Outside the door he stopped and poked his head inside.

"Surprise," he said cheerfully as he stepped inside the room and let his slacks fall in a bundle around his ankles.

Furious movement from beneath the sheets and his smile quickly faded. She wasn't alone.

"Oh, my God!" Allison screamed as she sat upright against the headboard and pulled the comforter up around her neck. "Gary... what are you doing..."

Before she could finish he cut her off. "What am I doing?" he sputtered, his voice raised to a hysterical pitch. "I think the better question is what are *you* doing? Or should I ask *who* are you doing?"

"Gary, honey ..."

"D-don't honey me," Gary stammered as he made his way across the room to their bed. "Who do you have under there, huh? Who's the lucky fellow?" He pulled back the sheets and tossed them in a heap on the floor. His jaw dropped at the sight of the naked body lying prone between his wife's legs. Tara Van Dyke looked as pretty as ever as she rolled over and smiled weakly at him.

52

The Big One

The initial shock melted away quickly, like an ice cube in the sun. Then, the room started spinning all around him and he had to sit down on the edge of the bed. This couldn't be happening, he thought. It had to be a bad dream. From behind him, Allison's voice assured him that what was happening was all too real.

"Honey, I'm so sorry about this," she mumbled softly as she reached out and touched his arm.

Gary pulled away quickly. "Don't. Don't touch me." He glanced over his shoulder at Allison, and then over to Tara who sat against the headboard with the comforter pulled up over her breasts. "How long has this been going on?"

Tara looked away quickly. Despite her disheveled nest of dark hair, and the fact that she had just been performing oral sex on his wife, she looked good. Even better than she had back in college.

"A couple years," Allison finally sighed. "I'm so sorry. I've been meaning to tell you, but I just didn't know how to bring it up. Honest, Gary. I'm telling you the truth."

"Allison's right," Tara added. "This has been going on for a while. We've both wanted to tell you. How do you bring something like this up though?"

Gary stood from the bed and walked to the window. Outside, beneath the perch of their condo, the day simmered with the usual activity. Cars zipping to and fro up and down the hilly avenues; pedestrians bustling down the sidewalks, some to appointments and meetings, others simply wandering aimlessly; trolleys following lines of track stitched into the fabric of the street. Out there, beyond the suddenly claustrophobic confines of his bedroom, life went on as normal for the rest of the world. In here, though, his world had been turned upside down.

"I don't really know what to think about all of this," he muttered, shaking his head as he continued staring out past the window. "I don't know…"

"It doesn't have to be a bad thing," Tara spoke from the bed. "I mean, life is too short to not enjoy it."

"Is that what you call this?" Gary fluster-queried. He turned and faced both women. "Enjoying life?"

"Gary, listen," Allison interjected, "I'm so sorry things worked out this way. I never wanted to hurt you. But I can't go on living a lie anymore. Tara and I, we really care for each other. But…"

He looked her directly in the eye. "But what?" An oily mix of anger and confusion tinged the periphery of his words.

Allison met his gaze. "I care for you too. What would you think about trying something new in our marriage?"

A puzzled look crossed his face, and then dissolved an instant later. "Are you suggesting what I think you're suggesting?"

Allison nodded sheepishly. She glanced at Tara and then back at Gary.

"I'm in if he is." Tara's lips curled into a mischievous smirk.

Another wave of shock rolled over him. This was all too much to digest at once. He stood and turned to leave, but stopped abruptly. He thought for a moment. What was that old saying? Something about looking a gift horse in the mouth.

"Sure," Gary finally shrugged as he tugged off his shirt. "Why not?"

Before crawling onto the bed the slight trembling beneath his feet went unnoticed. Had he felt it he probably would have chalked it up to nervous anticipation, and not a prelude to the end of his life.

• • •

Two miles beneath the slippery threesome on Bentley Street, the Pacific tectonic plate pushed against the North American plate, grinding together the two colossal land masses with enough force to alter ever so slightly the earth's rotational wobble. One plate moved south the other eased north, tearing at the eight-hundred-mile-long scar of the San Andreas Fault that ran from Hollister to Los Angeles.

On the streets of San Francisco, earthquake veterans barely even noticed the earth's movement. A slight bit of swaying and shaking, followed by a quiet lull. Just a minor temblor, everyone thought. After a few moments of stillness it started up again, slowly at first, barely noticeable. Only this time, the shaking didn't ease. Like a rogue wave it kept building, harder, faster, more violent with each passing second. Then, as the full force of *The Big One* finally hit with the stored energy of a million Hiroshima-sized nuclear bombs, all hell broke loose.

5931709R0

Made in the USA
Charleston, SC
22 August 2010